The Roots of CONCERN

The Roots of
CONCERN

Writings on Anabaptist Renewal
1952–1957

Edited by
Virgil Vogt

CASCADE *Books* • Eugene, Oregon

THE ROOTS OF CONCERN
Writings on Anabaptist Renewal 1952–1957

Copyright © 2009 Wipf and Stock Publishers. All rights reserved. Except for brief quotations in critical publications or reviews, no part of this book may be reproduced in any manner without prior written permission from the publisher. Write: Permissions, Wipf and Stock Publishers, 199 W. 8th Ave., Suite 3, Eugene, OR 97401.

Cascade Books
A Division of Wipf and Stock Publishers
199 W. 8th Ave., Suite 3
Eugene, OR 97401

www.wipfandstock.com

ISBN 13: 978-1-59752-189-5

Cataloging-in-Publication data:

The roots of CONCERN : writings on Anabaptist renewal 1952–1957 / Edited by Virgil Vogt.

xiv + 198 p. ; 23 cm. —Includes bibliographical references.

ISBN 13: 978-1-59752-189-5

1. Anabaptists—History—20th century. 2. Anabaptists—theology. I. Vogt, Virgil, 1934–. II. Peachey, Paul, 1918–. III. Yoder, John Howard. IV. Title.

BX8122. R60 2009

Manufactured in the U.S.A.

Contents

Foreword by Virgil Vogt • *vii*

The Historical Genesis of the *Concern* Project by Paul Peachey • *xi*

The Original Frontispiece of *Concern* Volumes 1–4 • *xiii*

Volume 1—1954

Introduction by Paul Peachey • 1

Toward an Understanding of the Decline of the West • 5
PAUL PEACHEY

The Anabaptist Dissent: The Logic of the Place of the Disciple in Society • 29
JOHN HOWARD YODER

Volume 2—1955

Preface by Paul Peachey • 45

The Church in the Old Testament • 47
JOHN W. MILLER

Spirit and Form in the Church of Christ • 57
PAUL PEACHEY

Biblicism and the Church • 67
DAVID A. SHANK AND JOHN HOWARD YODER

APPENDIX: Close Communion—On What Lines? 102

Volume 3—1956

Preface by Paul Peachey • 107

Intimations of Another Way: A Progress Report • 109
C. NORMAN KRAUS AND JOHN W. MILLER

Preaching in the Church? • 122
HANS-JOACHIM WIEHLER

A Concern Retreat • 129
J. LESTER BRUBAKER AND SOL YODER

The Call: Journal of Spiritual Reformation • 136
LEWIS BENSON

Notes on Books • 140

Volume 4—1957

Preface by Paul Peachey • 143

Epistolary: An Exchange by Letter • 145

What Is CONCERN? • 158
PAUL PEACHEY

What Are Our Concerns? • 164
JOHN HOWARD YODER

Organization and Church • 177
JOHN W. MILLER

Property: A Problem in Christian Ethics • 185
HERBERT KLASSEN

Foreword

Concern: Aspiring to a More Radical Christianity

The impulse to a more radical and authentic expression of Christian life is amazingly persistent in Anabaptist-Mennonite history. You see this reflected in the lives of some individual Mennonites. It can also be seen in similar renewal movements that arise from time to time from Mennonite soil.

The *Concern* movement among North American Mennonites—in middle of the last century—was certainly one of these "more radical" stirrings. The Anabaptist movement began as the radical wing of the sixteenth-century Protestant Reformation in Europe. And this radical impulse has been part of the Mennonite DNA ever since.

Mennonite leaders in the first half of the twentieth century were busy rediscovering the vitality of the early Anabaptists. But by midcentury, a younger generation of leaders thought that the rediscovered Anabaptist vision should translate into more radical versions of church life and Christian discipleship.

Seven of these young leaders were in Europe during the early 1950s, doing what bright, young Mennonites were supposed to do—preparing themselves for service in the church by getting the best possible graduate education in European universities, and working in Mennonite relief and reconstruction programs as Europe sought to recover from a devastating world war.

This group included Irvin B. Horst, John W. Miller, Paul Peachey, Calvin Redekop, David A. Shank, Orley Swartzentruber, and John Howard Yoder. They were devoted to the Christian vision as presented among North American Mennonites of the time. But their tasks in Europe brought them face to face with the great moral and spiritual dilemmas of the modern world.

These seven men are symbolic of the struggles of the entire North American Mennonite movement. That is why their writings touched a sensitive nerve within the broader church. The appearance of the first few issues of *Concern*, starting in 1952, caused quite a stir.

However, the seven *Concern* founders did not launch a continuing movement that others could join. They had not worked out a credible, sustainable plan for addressing the issues about which they voiced concern. But the pamphlets kept coming. The final one, *Concern* 18, was published in 1971. Nevertheless, the dialogue that this *Concern* group began has borne significant fruit, and it continues in some form to this present time. This dialogue centers on several major issues.

First, the *Concern* members were keen to point out the folly of trying to combine church and state in the manner begun by Emperor Constantine, which continued broadly through the remaining centuries of church history. Trying to impose Christian values on the state or using government to impose Christian values on the general population results in diminishing rather than increasing the moral impact of the gospel. *Concern* writers sought to recapture the vitality of the biblical vision of letting the church be the church and letting the world be the world. This separation of church and state may, in fact, be one of the most profound aspects of the Anabaptist movement of the sixteenth century.

The lukewarm quality of individual discipleship and Christian community life in the average North American church was also a matter of deep concern to these young Mennonite leaders. Christianity often appeared to be nothing more than a kind of religious veneer. In the substantive investment of time and energy, as well as in the values guiding major life decisions, Christians often seemed to differ very little from their secular and unbelieving counterparts. Had the salt of the earth lost its flavor?

Also of concern was the role of denominational organizations and centers of leadership. By using culturally approved ways of organizing, funding and mobilizing the work of the church, were the very institutions which helped to recall the history of the early Anabaptists actually leading Mennonite churches towards greater cultural accommodation? Was the language of Anabaptism being used to facilitate mainline Protestant adaptation? Was a more radical discipleship being fanned into flame, or just being watered down?

These concerns, which sparked the entire pamphlet series, were most clearly articulated in the first four pamphlets. They are reprinted here in one combined volume, giving us a penetrating glimpse into the evolving heart of North American Mennonite thinking nearly a half-century ago.

The search for a more radical and authentic version of Christian experience goes on because the impulse to do so certainly comes from God. The recurring appearance of renewal movements throughout Christian history is a tangible witness to the reality of a risen Lord Jesus Christ who personally directs these efforts.

What does it mean to live as children of God in a world that has lost its way?

Virgil Vogt
Reba Place
2006

[Publisher's note: Virgil Vogt served as the managing editor for *Concern* from the late 1950s to its culmination in the early 1970s. Readers new to these writings might benefit from beginning with material in Volume 4, escecially 158–76.]

The Historical Genesis of the CONCERN Project

The tinder, ample and dry, lay waiting. The spark was a conversation between two former student colleagues, who were then separated for five years by the Atlantic Ocean. Meeting again in Europe in the fall of 1951, they were surprised at the differences that had emerged between them. A wider consultation was needed, and readily ignited in the spring of 1952. But that the *Concern* flame would spring up was unimagined. "God moves in mysterious ways."

World War II, and its shattered aftermath, triggered the eleven-day meeting in Amsterdam of seven American Mennonite graduate students. Most of us had interrupted our graduate studies to join emergency services of our church agencies in postwar Europe. While two in the group had arrived soon after war's end, the others had come later. Exposed as we now were to raw edges of the recent war, we found ourselves overwhelmed. The imagery and procedures we brought from home had been proving inadequate.

Profound agreement emerged readily at Amsterdam, but so also did disagreement! The agreement can be described as triangular. One angle was the unsuitability of some policies engineered solely at Akron, Pennsylvania, the home office. Another angle was the ineptness of some doctrinal and ecclesial claims. The fundamental angle, however, was the recognition of the primacy of the cellular process (Matt 18:20) in what we call church life. Disagreement in part reflected the differing career paths on which we found ourselves; that is, in no way were we ready to unite in a new sectarian formation. (By 1957 our different career paths took us individually to five different countries on three continents. Regular meetings of the "Amsterdam Seven" ended.)

At the end of the of the Amsterdam meeting, we concluded that we needed to talk further. Hence a year later, we met again, this time in Zurich, Switzerland. There the notion emerged once more that we needed to converse further and more widely. The publication of "occasional papers" appeared as the appropriate form. In the implementation of that decision, the vehicle of the *Concern* pamphlet series emerged, effectively expressing our above agreements. Elaboration of two oral presentations during the second week at Amsterdam would become *Concern* No. 1, consisting of "Toward an Understanding of the Decline of the West" as backdrop for "The Anabaptist Dissent: The Logic of the Place of the Disciple in Society."

Particularly in the latter paper, church as dialogical gatherings of believing disciples versus its "identification with the whole of society" was hailed. *Concern* No. 2, with three articles, effectively elaborates pamphlet No. 1, and especially the second of the above papers, "The Anabaptist Dissent."

Concern No. 3 presents four papers by six writers—two papers co-authored—all but one by "outsiders," disclosing thus the widening circle of readers coming on board. One of the papers reports on a *Concern* retreat at Camp Luz in Ohio in 1956, the first such meeting held stateside. Another paper came from the leader of a comparable initiative in the Quaker community, in dialogue with *Concern*. *Concern* No. 4, responding in part to No. 3, came five years after the Amsterdam gathering.

Bracing though this episode may have been for those who participated, it was but one of countless revivals in the course of Christian history. The "routinization of the charisma" (Max Weber) recurs relentlessly as we falsely replace God's dynamic agency in our "world" with our own merely symbolic contrivances. Even our Bible reading can turn into mere idolatry. Why cannot we, in our responses as Christians, surmount that inclination? "No one has ever seen God; if we love one another, God lives in us, and his love is perfected in us" (1 John 4:12).

Paul Peachey
Harrisonburg, VA
2006

Original Frontispiece

CONCERN
A Pamphlet Series

Published by:

Irvin B. Horst
Koningslaan 58
Amsterdam, Netherlands

John W. Miller
1407 S. Eighth St.
Goshen, Indiana

Paul Peachey
Eastern Mennonite College
Harrisonburg, Virginia

Calvin Redekop
Hesston College
Hesston, Kansas

David A. Shank
14, Avenue de la Brabanconne
Brussels, Belgium

Orley Swartzentruber
10, Rue Jeane Hachette
Clamart (Seine), France

John Howard Yoder
Binningerstr. 83, Allschwiel
Basel, Switzerland

Editorial note:
Concern is an independent pamphlet series dealing with current Mennonite and general Christian issues. Its character is semi-popular and is designed to stimulate informal discussion and common searching within the brotherhood for a strengthening of prophetic Christian faith and conduct. The publishers share responsibility for the publication in general, but since articles are published for the sake of study and discussion, they do not purport to be definitive nor does the editorial group necessarily concur in every detail.

(The text above appeared on the inside cover of all four of the first *Concern* pamphlets.)

. . . send me to Judah, to the city of my fathers' sepulchres, that I may rebuild it.
—Nehemiah (Neh 2:5)

If any man would come after me, let him deny himself and take up his cross daily and follow me. For whoever would save his life will lose it; but whoever loses his life for my sake, he will save it.
—Jesus (Luke 9:23–24)

Modern Christianity is degenerating because it has been relegated to a corner of the human soul and ceased to be a totalitarian attitude towards life.
—N. Berdyaev (*Towards a New Epoch*, Geoffrey Bles, London, 1949, p. 106)

VOLUME 1

1954

INTRODUCTION by Paul Peachey

World War II brought the far corners of the earth to America's doorsteps. In its homes, shops, and streets, people discussed Iwo Jima, Dakar, and St. Lo as though they were neighboring villages over the next hill. To pacifist groups, whose young men were confined to American shores during the conflict, this transformation of the wide world into a familiar neighborhood did not come until the cessation of hostilities. Since then, probably fifteen hundred American Mennonites have sailed the seven seas or flown the world's skyways.

The American Mennonite relief effort, which occasioned the major portion of this travel, was in its own way a miracle. Farm families, some of whom could hardly distinguish Europe from the Orient, planted, cooked, and sewed for the world's anonymous suffering millions. For our churches (and others like them), this effort was an enriching new experience in which we learned something of the "twice-blest" quality of mercy.

In another sense, however, the challenge of the postwar period revealed deep inadequacies in the spiritual resources within our brotherhood. In the first acute years of postwar disillusionment, among victor and vanquished alike, when the spiritual conflict continued unabated, and in new forms as rival forces struggled for the possession of men's souls, we were unable to define or to communicate the message that seemed implicit in our professed position. Those to whom the privilege came to enter deeply into the foreign relief program found their souls abundantly enlarged by the experience, but at the same time, many of us were perplexed by this larger failure. And this perplexity was only increased when we turned, in terms of these experiences abroad, to reevaluate the Christian tradition of which we were a part. On the one hand, the great catastrophe that had befallen Europe, that proud and cultured custodian of Christianity for many centuries, confirmed our conviction that the "gathered" pattern of Christian community, rediscovered by our sixteenth-century ancestors, is indeed the real intent of the Gospel. On the other hand, the strengthening of this conviction could only intensify our concern over the partial sterility of our efforts at home and abroad. What we in effect proclaimed as an answer for people in devastated countries was no longer a dynamic transforming leaven in our own midst.

It was these experiences that led together the group responsible for the present publication in Amsterdam during the post-Easter season of 1952 and again at the same period of 1953 in Zürich. We are American Mennonites who for the most part had at that time already spent several years in Christian service in Europe and had done graduate work at European universities. Through fellowship and common searching and the stimulation of a few guest speakers, we hope to take stock of our experiences and position.

The respective themes of these conferences were: "The Decline of the West" and "Anabaptism and Eschatology," themes which against the backdrop of a Europe in tremors were urgently real. Not many miles removed were the festering wounds of super-militarism—cities still in rubble, the flotsam of refugees and derelict, and acres of sprawling army camps prepared for new conflagrations. Still more revealing was by way of contrast the spiritual enervation of an Amsterdam or Zürich, where the spiritual desert is boarded up by Western traditions and pride.[1]

---

1. Publisher's note: in the original publication of this material the author quoted an excerpt from T. S. Eliot's poem *The Waste Land*.

In a setting marked by strong contrasts, then, it is not surprising that a frame of mind which posed issues in contrasts characterized these meetings. On the one hand we were aware of the more complete discipleship of the early Christians coupled with a fervent expectancy of the *parousia*, and on the other, of our own compromised life and at-home-ness in the world. In a similar vein we sensed the validity of the Anabaptist dissent and "exodus" as over against world conformity within church life conterminous with society, freedom and necessity as expressed in the pneumatic church versus conformity and organization in the institutional church, and the renewal and perpetuation of the true Christian community as compared to a church which becomes traditional or justifies the process of assimilation.

Nevertheless, despite the weaknesses which we sensed acutely, we felt a deep loyalty and gratitude to the brotherhood which has nourished us and to which we belong by choice. It was precisely this loyalty which impelled our search and made us critically sensitive to decay and inconsistency where they exist. And so the question arose, a question still unanswered: Are American Mennonites, in spite of their great institutional and even spiritual progress, perhaps after all moving rather toward "respectable" denominationalism rather than toward a dynamic and prophetic "grass roots" movement? And if so, what responsibility devolves upon us in our generation?

That we venture to publish a few introductory excerpts from these discussions is no indication that we feel that we have found answers to these questions. Indeed, the decision to publish was reached only after long deliberation. The papers themselves, prepared as they were in the midst of other pressing duties, made no pretense of scholarly thoroughness, but were rather interpretive essays on experiences and observations along the way, designed as bases for study and discussion. In the present publication two papers are being released for limited circulation among persons interested in the issues raised. Subsequent articles will deal with more specific issues in accordance with developing discussion.

Finally, we know full well that we, too, are a part of our proud Western civilization, that we are no better than our fellow Christians. But perhaps the past several decades will have taught us Christians to be *pessimistic* about their surrounding culture but *optimistic* about the Church of Christ. In Europe and America, in the Orient and the Occident, in our beloved church as well as in other communions, the

Lord calls those who will come. Such elect belong neither to the East nor to the West but are citizens of God's kingdom and members of the transnational commonwealth of Christ. We need not despair, for he who discovers the things of this world perishing before his eyes and his soul not bound to them finds freedom and joy which will help him face any circumstances of the future. At least he realizes that he is in league with God, that he no longer belongs to the order of this world, that the *Civitas Dei* is neither in Rome nor Geneva, neither in Moscow nor Washington—but eternal in the heavens.

Toward an Understanding of the Decline of the West

PAUL PEACHEY

I

The western world was ushered into the present century by the optimistic philosophy of the evolutionary progress of the processes of history. Science and technology had overcome so many of the incongruities of human existence that it seemed to be only a matter of time until the paradise of which men in all ages had dreamed would become reality on earth. What philosophers proclaimed seemed confirmed on every hand by the solid achievements of the human genius. The ascent from the lower to the higher, which in the philosophy of medieval scholasticism had required at every transitional stage a transcendent creative intervention, was now seemingly being achieved by the pulsations of immanent energy.

Today, at mid-century, that same western world grovels uneasily beneath the ruins of its utopia, trembling with fear of even worse things to come. In Europe this fear seems to have produced among many a general apathy toward life and the future, while in America one sees symptoms of panic and malaise. The difference in reaction, however, is only that Europe has already progressed further along the road of disillusionment. For the confidence of Europe was shaken already by World War I—indeed she had premonitions before that time of terrible things to come—while only with

World War II and the Korean conflict did the terrible truth come home to America. Furthermore, Europe has experienced the catastrophe in her own flesh and blood while America knows it only theoretically in terms of the terror she herself produced at Dresden and Hiroshima. Some European observers detected the first tremors of fear in America between 1945 and 1950 when her conscience showed the first signs of uneasiness because of the bomb she had unleashed and the realization dawned that the achievement of world order lay beyond her powers, a realization that the stalemate of Korea, America's first un-won war, can only deepen.

The spirit of despair found its European prophet already during the interwar period in Oswald Spengler, the despondent German philosopher who published his dirge for Western civilization under the title, *Der Untergang des Abendlandes—The Decline of the West*. His theories gave expression to the despondent feelings of many intellectuals who believed that the civilization of the West had run its course. World War II has increased the speculation as to the significance of the crisis, particularly in Germany, who out of her own experience knows perhaps better than any other western nation its dimensions. In widely different circles, today's conditions have come to be regarded as the end stage of secularization and de-Christianization. By contrast the Middle Ages now appear as the age of faith. People yearn for the security of cultural unity and harmony which medieval times offered, as can be seen in the resurgence of the Catholic Church in many areas and in the pilgrimage into her fold of certain classes of people, particularly European poets and prose writers. Parallel to this is the swing toward orthodoxy, the rise of a strong liturgical trend, and the self-contradictory reawakening of confessional consciousness in many quarters within the Protestant world. Indeed one can note striking similarities to the restorative and romantic period which followed the French Revolution and the Napoleonic Wars.

The interpretation given this crisis in western civilization varies greatly according to the viewpoint of the observer. Catholicism as the exponent of cultural unity under the tutelage of the church naturally regards it as the consequence and the final stage of man's revolt against God, against His church, and against Christ's vicar on earth. Where they are not engulfed in the humanist stream the reaction of the "official" Protestant bodies often does not differ greatly from the Catholic, since they too pose as the spiritual guardians of society. The secular humanist[2] viewpoint arrives at opposite conclusions, for it denies that the Middle Ages were ever as thoroughly Christian as the proponents of Christian culture would have it, and would at any rate never assign religion as important a role in the affairs of men as it is accorded by the religious traditions themselves. A third viewpoint is that of evangelical Christians, who find themselves divided, however, between the approach of the Catholics and that of the humanists. Some would agree with the former that the process of secularization is responsible for the crisis, but would view the whole in the perspective of an intense eschatological schematization, while others would agree strangely enough with the humanists that medieval society never had been thoroughly Christianized, and consequently would feel that today's crisis in a stricter sense is not merely the secularization of world culture.

It is a common characteristic of all schools of thought, however, to hold that evil forces threaten to reduce to ashes at a single blow the accumulated cultural heritage of painfully progressing centuries. All seem to agree that an old epoch in human history has passed but that a stable foundation for a new one has not yet been laid. Nevertheless the majority of men cling tenaciously to the remnants of the old order, determined to preserve its privileges and unable to face the sacrificial demands of a new unformed era. Indeed no one, whatever his persuasion, can contemplate with complacency the outbreak of new wars or revolutions. Alone the communist votaries of revolution relish the thought of catastrophe, and in western countries few of them realize what they worship.

II

It is the purpose of this paper to examine briefly this belief that the West is in a state of decline and to suggest elements essential to a Christian attitude toward the problem. To analyze Western history and civilization

---

2. The term "humanist" is used in this paper to refer broadly to the various modern streams of secular thought, beginning with the Renaissance. These streams of thought manifest in varying degrees the following characteristics: they repudiate special revelation and/or subordinate its authority to reason and empiricism and seek to explain man and the universe in terms of immanent energy and processes. Thus in the name of "immanence" they stand in opposition to transcendental (i.e., ultimately revealed) truth and are actually "man-centered" or "humanistic."

in this light is a stupendous task, as the widely differing conclusions of men who have spent their lifetime studying it amply testify. I make no pretense of having begun to master the mass of material that needs to be studied, to say nothing of the inscrutability of the ways of God in history. Indeed, preoccupation with questions as these whose larger dimensions lie beyond human comprehension can lead to futile speculation which will deflect the Christian from his main responsibility to live and proclaim the Gospel within history, content to leave the larger meanings to God. It can tempt men to seek for human remedies and to rely on manmade devices, forgetting that human destiny ultimately lies in the hand of God. Furthermore, all historical writing and all cultural analysis is of necessity selective, interpretative, and insofar subjective, so that salient facts may completely escape notice. Finally, one must note the errors which historical consciousness has brought into Western thought and even into the church, such as philosophies of history which have deified the process of history itself. But bearing in mind all these and other dangers, we cannot escape the problems which our time thrusts upon us. Without understanding in some fashion at least the age in which we live, we cannot hope either to survive as a gathered Christian group nor yet to fulfill the task of Christian witnessing. This paper, however, is not based on any exhaustive or systematic study; it simply constitutes reflections made along the way, and is offered as a contribution to a discussion which I hope will be continuous and will help to give us the orientation which we need to fulfill the responsibilities of our own generation.

III

The term, "decline of the West" presupposes a previous level of attainment now in the process of disintegration. The "West" which is here meant is European civilization primarily, but including also its American extension, which civilization is the creation of medieval Catholicism and of fifteenth- to twentieth-century humanism. While now one, now the other, is given the major credit for the total structure, depending on the viewpoint of the observer, in either case it seems clear that not only the civilization itself but also the presuppositions upon which it rested are threatened. An examination of these two great cultural forces will therefore be necessary.

Medieval Society as the *Corpus Christianum*

Historians have traditionally divided Western history into three periods: ancient, medieval, and modern. While the roots of Europe go deep into the ancient past, and consequently have fed on various traditions, particularly the Greek and the Latin, Europe as we know it today is seen as the creation of medieval times. After the ancient empires one after the other were broken up, the Romans emerged shortly before the birth of Christ to achieve the imperial political unity of the Mediterranean world. Local religions and cultures had failed and a great process of eclecticism and synthesization had set in. The failure of the Greek gods to protect the great civilization of Greece had discredited them and led to a decline in the importance of religion as a factor in the affairs of men. Thus Christ brought His message to the world at a time when an optimum of transnational stability had been reached, while the resistance of competing religions was remarkably low.

In the mind of Christian historians, this coincidence of the coming of Christ with a maximum of political stability and a minimum of cultural resistance constitutes in part "the fullness of the time" of which the prophets predicting the coming of Christ had spoken. Nevertheless the tide was soon to turn inasmuch as the religious indifference lasted only several centuries, for not only did the Roman emperors now seek to unify the empire by means of an imperial religion such as Mithraism, but the third and fourth centuries of our era were marked by what Professor Marrou of Paris has called a new religiosity. New credibility was attached to the intervention of the gods in the affairs of men, after several centuries marked by skepticism. But now, once Christianity had gained a real entree among the Mediterranean peoples, demanding as it did the ultimate loyalty of its adherents, a conflict with the absolute demands of the empire and its gods was inevitable. This led to persecutions till Constantine with political astuteness recognized in Christianity the greatest spiritual force in his empire and reversing the policy of suppression, enlisted its support in the imperial achievement.

Constantine is usually regarded as a turning point in the history of the church and of the West, but the actual compromise of which he is the symbol was a process that far superseded his span of life, a process in which the church and the empire as universal concepts became coterminous. Nevertheless, when the barbaric storms descended on Rome, Christianity was still a vital force, sufficiently autonomous that when the empire fell, it survived, despite the accusation of pagan Romans to the contrary that it had caused the downfall of the eternal city. As Augustine—who became the leading theologian for the post-Constantine centuries—fended off the pagan accusations, he defined the church as the transcendent *Civitas Dei*, and by a slight misinterpretation the Roman church as an institution identified herself with the *Civitas*, with the millennium of Christ, and for a thousand years medieval Europe lived under the illusion that the millennium could be realized within history.

Until the fall of Rome (A.D. 476) the chief cultural forces at work in the empire had been the Greek, i.e., Hellenist, and Latin traditions, now in interaction with Christianity. The entrance of the Germanic peoples into the Latin world brought the fourth great component of European civilization into the picture. In a remarkable fusion of cultures, these uncivilized peoples coming from the North were to inherit the political tradition and responsibility of the empire while at the same time yielding to the cultural superiority of the Mediterranean peoples. It was as the Mediterranean culture, particularly the "Christianized" Latin, was carried northward across the Alps and assimilated by the Germanic tribes that modern Europe was born. The original heirs of the Roman tradition were the Franks, who occupied finally the area between the Loire and the Rhine rivers. But on into the heart of modern Germany, in thousands of small clearings in the dark Teutonic forests, courageous missionary monks planted sanctuaries and slowly chiseled away at the raw blocks of savagery to create eventually the modern European spirit.

The classic theologian of this Europe was Thomas Aquinas. On the skeleton of Aristotelian philosophy he erected a magnificent structure of thought, founded upon the unified authority of natural and revealed theology, embracing the totality of human experience and able to absorb within itself all the incongruous and contradictory in the world of men. In this great system the lower was only a preliminary stage to the higher. Every line strove forever upward as did architectural lines of the Gothic cathedral which this great culture produced. No state was so lowly, no function so menial, that it had no place in the providence of God, to enhance His eternal glory. On all the disharmonious, the imperfect, the suffering, the church as the extension of the incarnation radiated by way of the sacraments the Eternal Presence. Even kings and emperors were thought to have been brought under the reign of Christ, and the tension between church and world had disappeared. Day and night monastic voices and the incense of worship ascended in anticipation and imitation of the multitudes that shall assemble around the throne of God to sing His praises eternally. At the head of this great divine-human society stood the vicar of Christ, representing and safeguarding His seamless robe. The *corpus christianum* was indeed the most magnificent dream ever dreamed by man.

The actual accomplishments of this great system were impressive, both religiously and culturally, and remain so to this day. In the first place, the cults of paganism were successfully eradicated, despite remnants which remain to this day, and monotheism was everywhere established. Theism became the worldview of the West, and the religious consciousness affected profoundly the political concepts of the time. Christian theology, literature, symbols, and liturgy were introduced, and once the Holy Scriptures were in Europe a recurrent eruption of Gospel freshness was assured. In the second place, Christianity brought not only a new religion but a new ethic. However imperfectly its ideals may have been realized in practice, no one in Europe could escape its influence. The religious unrest of the late Middle Ages and the flourishing of mysticism, both of which were the soil from which the Reformation sprang, testify to the success of medieval Catholicism in educating the Germanic conscience. In the third place, the impulse of Christianity as it fused with the undifferentiated genius of northern Europe produced a new culture far superior to any culture previously known. Indeed it was the spirit of Christianity that eventually pulled Europe from the "Dark Ages" which succeeded the collapse of the ancient Roman Empire.

Nevertheless the medieval vision, the *corpus christianum*, was doomed from the outset. In the first place, the Christianity which penetrated north of the Alps was no longer pure. Already the mere fact that it was carried by monks who, despite the Christian heroism that characterized their work, were an aberration of the Gospel ideal, could only mean that a distorted social ethic reached the pagan tribesman. In the very process of evangelism itself, important concessions were made to the pagan spirit. So Pope Gregory the Great (590–604) instructed the great Benedictine missionary Augustine, who was sent to the Angles, to simply sanctify by means of holy water the heathen sanctuaries already in existence so as to win the pagans more readily. Even their festivals were to be transformed into Christian feasts: "For if a few outer pleasures are left to them they will be more quickly attracted by the inner joys. For to cut off everything from these hard hearts at one blow is without doubt impossible. He who wishes to scale a high mountain can do so only with slow steps, not by leaps." We cannot here discuss the question of missionary technique with illiterate pagan peoples. It is important only to note the discolored Christian message which reached the Teutonic world. More disastrous than all else, however, was the debasement of Christianity which stemmed from the Constantinian compromise, for not only had state and church become united, not only was Christianity now falsely captivated by and identified with the culture of the Occident, but it had become a mere means to mundane ends. Throughout all human history, natural religion has always been the highest cohesive and integrative force in any society and culture, as the numerous studies of "primitive" peoples made in our century have shown. This is precisely what Christianity is not. As Jacob Burckhardt, the great Swiss historian, points out, the Christian religion, in contrast to the polytheistic cults of classical paganism, "was and is not a cult consecrating a national culture but a transcendent faith in a future redemption. It was hostile to the pagan gods of nature and culture, as it must be hostile to the idols of modern civilization." But Christianity was now no longer primarily the redemptive intervention of God, but a new means to cultural and political ends, subservient to the caprice of the ruling caste.

In the second place, the basic presuppositions of the *corpus christianum* were false. The Gospel speaks to men who are morally free to reject its claims. Everywhere it recognizes that some will accept while others will reject its message. And while the universality of its intent and of the final triumph of Christ is nonetheless upheld, the Gospel nowhere visualizes a permanent peace between "church" and "world," nowhere predicts the final harmonization of all that is incongruous in human experience except eschatologically, and nowhere promises the redemption of this aeon in toto. Thus Jesus had to declare Himself: "I am not come to send peace but a sword." To set up an ecclesiastical and political regime that presupposed that the totality of mankind had been embraced within the Christian community could therefore never correspond with reality.

In the third place, the *corpus christianum* even as an ideal was possible only as long as the theistic worldview was universally acknowledged. Men might not necessarily accept the claims of Christianity existentially—indeed the recognition of supernatural reality is not a uniquely Christian insight—but as long as the mythological worldview of medieval man, which was in part a continuation of pre-Christian theologies, persisted, there was no escape from the external demands of the church-dominated society. Once, however, modern discoveries disenchanted or demythologized the world, and man began to feel himself autonomous and free from dependence on deity, the whole structure was undermined. The only recourse open to the *corpus* at this point was to suppress coercively every dissent and cultural heterogeneity. But this was a basic contradiction of the essence of the Christian faith, which is at heart voluntaristic. Furthermore this confusion of a sort of natural or instinctive theism with the revealed Christian faith could only obscure the distinction between the providential and redemptive activities of God.

In the fourth place, the attempt of the church in medieval times to direct the whole of society necessarily plunged her into ethical compromise. The governance of unredeemed men requires measures and means that are fundamentally at variance with the essence of the Gospel. In the position of ethical compromise the Christian "salt" lost its "savour," the church her prophetic otherness that would have enabled her to rebuke and transform the abuses of society. All too soon she became so imbedded in the *status quo* that those who wished to rise higher came into conflict with her totalitarian claims and were mercilessly dealt with as heretics.

Finally, Christianity in Europe has never been too much more than a veneer, for the true Christians have always been in the minority. Many of the tribes were originally converted (read baptized) en masse. Beneath the new Christian traditions the old pagan stream continued to flow, ever ready to reappear under favorable circumstances. The men of the Third Reich could still establish contact with the old Germanic god, Wodan, ridiculous as it may seem. It is remarkable how frequently one finds the religious comprehension of the common people who have been "churched" for centuries limited to a vague, almost naturalistic, theism, which knows God primarily as Providence. Superstition is still widely prevalent, and many smaller traces of paganism still remain, such as certain festivals or practices as runic symbols on farm buildings, or local traditions as in Westphalia the "Heidenweck" (heathen bread rolls) used on Mardi Gras. That elements of the pre-Christian past should persist is neither surprising nor of itself disastrous. Indeed this demonstrates unmistakably the great task which the Gospel must undertake to transform us poor pagans into true sons of God. The error arose, however, in the assumption that the entire culture could be or had been Christianized, for Christianity now ceased to be prophetic.

The Modern Humanist Worldview

Despite the great achievements of his society, the lot of late medieval man was not a very happy one. Furthermore, by the late Middle Ages the creative force of the *corpus christianum* had been largely spent and new ideals began to stir his imagination. Whether or not the re-emergence of pagan impulses in the spirit of Western man as heralded by the Renaissance is to be attributed to the failure of the medieval church is not easy to determine and must at any rate remain an open question in the present discussion. In an article published several years ago in the German weekly, "Sonntagsblatt," published by Bishop Lilje, Nicholas Berdyaev asked, "Why did not the superior religious insights of the Middle Ages, and superior they were to both the ancient and the barbaric traditions, produce a Christian renaissance?" In his answer to his own question he pointed out that Christianity had introduced two principles into the experience of man: (1) the eschatological-messianic principle in which Christ has entered history, thereby ending the concept that history repeats itself in endlessly reproduced cycles, and revealing the purposeful movement of history toward a final goal and (2) the principle of freedom in history as over against the older idea of predetermination. Indeed it is this freedom that makes for movement in history as such. And it was the assertion of this freedom that made the Renaissance possible. Why then did Christianity not do it? Because, according to Berdyaev, Christianity had also introduced a conflict between these two principles, for the Middle Ages tried to realize the kingdom of God by coercion, thus denying to man that very freedom which the Gospel would effect.

The analysis of Berdyaev seems valid, and yet, proceeding as we are from a voluntaristic concept of Christianity, we can hardly make the church entirely responsible for the rise or fall of a civilization, nor can we assume a priori that the church could have retained the spiritual leadership of the modern scientific movement. To the extent, however, that the church employed non-Christian means in the suppression of dissent and presumed to dictate coercively the conduct of men who had rejected the central presuppositions of Christianity or of her claims, she herself drove men to revolt, once they discovered the hoax. In any event, the rediscovery of the ancients, the expansion of the geographic horizon of the late medieval world, the discovery of scientific experimentation and of certain elementary principles governing the functioning of the universe, which were not known before, introduced a spirit of doubt and inquiry into the Western mind that was to grow steadily till the twentieth century, and destroyed the theistic worldview to which Western civilization originally owed its existence. The full-blown humanist worldview, however, in certain respects differed little from the Thomist concept which preceded it. For modern humanism, whatever its particular philosophical expression, likewise visualized the attainment of paradise within history. As larger and larger areas of life were brought under rational control, as the old frontiers of human self-determination receded rapidly, and as humanity evolved steadily upward, it seemed only reasonable to believe that in time everything incongruous in human experience would be resolved, and all the discordant would be harmonized. The difference was that where the *corpus christianum* looked to the transcendent, the supernatural, for fulfillment, the humanist structure relied on the immanent, the natural. For Darwin and Thomas both, there was a gradual ascent from the lower forms of life to the higher. But where Thomas held that every transition required a supernatural, creative act, Darwin held that transition from the lower to the higher forms would be realized through immanent or innate energy. And if Thomism was far preferable to Darwinism because of its deference to the transcendent, i.e., to God, it shared with the latter its fatal misunderstanding of the provisional and contingent nature of the present aeon.

By the early sixteenth century people already dared to appeal to non-Christian authorities in their criticisms of existing conditions, religious as well as secular. Since then the world has become disenchanted. Where medieval man saw demons at work, modern man has discovered bacteria. Where medieval man saw the justice of God striking down the wicked, modern man sees the consequences of the violation of the laws of "nature." Where medieval man wrote off the unknown as lying enshrouded by the supernatural, modern man sees only unexplored vistas of the natural and the physical. Whatever inspiration the modern ideals of human dignity and freedom have drawn from Christian sources, modern man somehow feels that he owes the conveniences and comforts of modern life more to the empiricism of the doubting humanist than to the faith of the believing Christian. The pioneers of the physical sciences as Copernicus, Kepler, and Galileo were neither impelled by unbelief in their research nor led to it by their discoveries. The opposition of the church, however, both Catholic and Protestant, identified her with the forces of reaction, and more and more men found the Christian faith incompatible with the facts of science. The telling blows or medieval bigotry and religious intolerance were not dealt even by the Reformation, to say nothing of Catholicism, but by the secular Enlightenment. It was Voltaire who took up the cause of the persecuted Huguenots and nourished the spirit of toleration that went into the French declaration of "The Rights of Man and the Citizen." Even if in this particular case, the Catholics were persecuting Protestants, the latter were no better. In 1541 the Protestant government of Bern sent the nobleman Naegli to Paris to protest against the French government's suppression of the Huguenots at the same time that her own prisons were overflowing with Anabaptists. The reasons for persecution were identical.

Throughout the eighteenth and nineteenth centuries and on into the twentieth, the humanist stream continued to swell, as emancipated moderns reveled in their new freedom and power. Philosophers were busily hewing out new gods in place of the old One who had been left behind. First came the apotheosis of reason, then of evolution and progress, and, finally, of science and the machine. And the church, accustomed for a millennium to identify herself with the social regime in power, with the *status quo*, strove to maintain her privileges, either by political power as in Catholic countries or by adaptation in Protestant countries.

The grandeur of the humanist dream is not to be denied. That modern autonomous man, ostensibly in his own strength, "subdued the earth" to a degree never approached by a culture exclusively devoted to the supernatural gives him an unassailable dignity. And yet when all the accounts are rendered the picture changes profoundly, for not only was the humanist giant far more indebted to Christianity than he ever realized, but he misunderstood the basic human limitations and moral weakness even worse than medieval Catholicism had ever done.

Humanism's Indebtedness to Christianity

The modern humanist tradition has often been sternly critical of social injustice to which even Christians had all too often quietly acquiesced. We have already noted that religious tolerance in Europe was more or less a product of the Enlightenment. One might also point to Karl Marx and his associates, who, proceeding from a militantly materialistic worldview, drew the attention of the world to the abuses of British industry during the first half of the nineteenth century. And yet a closer examination of the great crusades for social justice reveals, particularly in England, that whatever secular idealists may have had to say about social injustice, the men who actually accomplished the slow and painful tasks of reform drew their inspiration largely from Christian sources. The men who finally killed the English slave trade and who drove the exploitation of woman and child labor from English factories had roots deep in the Methodist revival, many of them being lay preachers or sons of ministers. After World War II, American labor unions joined the coordinating council of American relief agencies which worked in Germany, unions which actually represented millions of workers, but it was the churches who did the main job. In a different way, the same thing might be said of the eighteenth- and nineteenth-century Continental prophets of human autonomy, whatever their specific philosophic persuasion. It was very often their orthodox or Pietist upbringing that prevented their drawing practical conclusions from their intellectual revolt. Immanuel Kant's ethical sternness is not primarily an organic part of his philosophy. It is much more a philosophic adaptation of a stern Scotch Presbyterian and German Pietist upbringing that had formed his early life.

The Misunderstanding of Humanism

The basic error of humanism, whatever its philosophic or scientific garb, has been the supposition that the unlocking of the mysteries of the universe, the gradual rationalization of life, and the supposed evolutionary ascent of the race would enable man himself to overcome the incongruities of human existence. It failed to see that technological and scientific or even philosophic progress, even though seemingly unlimited in potential development, could never alter a single strand of man's moral fiber, that, to the contrary, such progress increased the potential for evil as much as the potential for good, that the problem of evil as related to the human personality lies at the heart of the human enigma, and that consequently civilized man no more possesses the key to Paradise by the mere virtue of his knowledge than did his tribal forefathers.

It took the catastrophic wars of the twentieth century and the revolt of the oppressed to unmask the folly of the humanist dream. Not only did the wars in their external effects destroy the belief that by inherent forces man moved steadily upward, but the monstrosities of the totalitarian states revealed fully the autonomous man who was no longer inhibited as some of his forerunners had been by an inbred piety. The men of Dachau demonstrated in unmistakable terms how the fully autonomous human animal beneath a godless sky conducts himself. And when the nation which ostensibly was the real citadel of Christian virtue, something of a modern counterpart of the *corpus christianum*, unleashed on a defenseless city of women and children the first atomic bomb, the disillusionment of modern man was well-nigh complete. Meanwhile, the theoretical basis of scientism was equally shaken. The series of discoveries initiated by Albert Einstein's first formulation of the theory of Relativity in 1905 has gradually shattered the scientist's "absolute" laws of causality or determinacy, of the space-time categories, and the concept of the "closed universe" objectively measurable. We have thus witnessed in our generation the default of the humanist dream, a crisis perhaps equal in profundity to the failure of the medieval religious worldview at the dawn of the modern era.

IV

Our discussion to this point has dealt with two worldviews as having created and informed Western man: the medieval Christian and the modern humanist. What has been the contribution of Protestantism? For the average Protestant, Mennonites included, the Reformation is an event in Christian history second in significance only to the inception of Christianity itself. In terms of potential Christian achievement, of the breakthrough of the evangelical experience in Europe, of the shattering of Catholicism's false authority, and of the re-postulation of the authority of the Word of God and the community of the believers, this viewpoint seems well justifiable. To the Catholic, however, the Reformation appears as an episode in the process of the secularization of modern culture A good illustration of this viewpoint is Alois Beck's introduction to his *Messerklärung* (Mölding bei Wien, 1949), a German handbook to the Latin mass for the general public (Beck is the initiator of the contemporary Catholic Bible-reading campaign in German-speaking Europe), where he describes the secularization of the West as follows: "For about 500 years the Church has been defending herself against a world which has been becoming increasingly ungodly; the development began with the Nominalism of William of Occam; in the time of the *Reformation* a part of the Christians said *'No' to the Church* and separated itself from the pope; in the time of the *Enlightenment* there followed a *'No' to Christ*, while outwardly men still held to a 'world architect' (Deism, Free Masonry), who was, however, no longer concerned about anything; *during approximately the last century* this apostasy developed its logical last step: to a *'No' to God*, in whose place now some creature was deified: Technology and Progress, Blood and Soil, Power and Gold. Further from God it is not possible to go; we are thus standing at a spiritual turning point; the modern age with its rational darkness is dying."

In the realm of culture and social ethics I am increasingly inclined to concur with the Catholic view of the Reformation, though I draw far different conclusions of the case. The Reformation as such is difficult to isolate sufficiently from parallel movements and impulses in secular areas of life to permit an adequate analysis. As we have seen, Beck suggests that its roots lay in the rise of nominalism, a view shared by many others. It will be remembered that Luther's early theological development lay under the nominalist influence of William of Occam through the latter's disciple, Gabriel Biel of Tübingen. Others have seen the roots of the Reformation primarily in the Renaissance, which was largely true in the case of Zwingli, and quite generally so inasmuch as the humanists introduced the study of Scripture in the original tongues, and on the basis of Scripture dared to criticize existing religious conditions even counter to the authoritarian claims of the church. Again one might emphasize the importance of mysticism in late medieval society or the geographic and scientific discoveries which served to weaken the authority of the medieval church.

Whatever we decide about the origins of the Reform, we can regard it as a new and genuine answer to the Gospel by the Germanic conscience no longer able to accept the Catholic evangel. German Protestant scholars tend to regard the Reformation as the "acute Germanization of

Christianity," as the release of a new genius within the Christian tradition. And certainly any Protestant would agree that Luther's rediscovery of justification by faith was indeed a triumph of unending significance over centuries of accumulated distortion. The same could be said of the other two cardinal principles of the Reformation—the supreme authority of Scripture and the universal priesthood of believers. The Reform indeed brought a new day for the Christian Church.

Why then is the Protestant claim of the significance of the Reformation not justifiable? To me the simple answer seems to be that it mistakenly identifies the actual development of the Reformation with the personal experience and the ideals of the isolated Luthers. The unique thing about the Reformation was not that Luther's experience was so revolutionarily new—there had been religious awakenings before—but that it coincided with other latent forces, particularly nationalism which needed only the detonator that Luther's message provided in order to be set in motion. Already at the Council of Constance, a century earlier, the seamless robe of Christ had been rent by the new national gods. Now in the sixteenth century, that part of the Protestant message which caught the imagination of rulers and people alike was the proclamation of freedom, these from the Roman hegemony, those from the burdens of peasantry. Hence the Reformation can hardly be called a popular revival. On the local level it meant little actual change. Governments had to legislate on matters of simple morality, sometimes to take the wind out of the sails of the Anabaptists, since on the popular level a quickening of the conscience did not result. Luther's later years were enveloped in gloom because the Reform had failed to produce the piety and morality among the masses for which he had hoped.

The new spiritual impulses which the Reform actually generated were choked out by the old concept of cultural homogeneity, by the social order of the *corpus christianum*, which persisted and was accepted by the leading Reformers. Thus the Reformation failed to sense and to challenge the central error of Catholicism with regard to the essence of the church and her relationship to society. Despite new formulations which were designed to remedy some of the evils of the system, the basic presupposition of medieval times—that the borders of the church were coextensive with the entire society, while membership was effected, not by personal decision and commitment but by external coercion and clerically administered sacrament—was too deeply imbedded in the subconscious stream of European thought to be seriously challenged. In the religious struggles and wars which followed in the century after the Reformation, it was not the persecution of believers by the "world," but the rivalry of two systems both laying claim to inclusive totality. Wilhelm Dilthey, a German philosopher of the turn of the century, in his analysis of the worldview of the Renaissance and the Reformation, concludes that the Reformation was not a restoration of primitive Christianity but rather a further development of the medieval universal ideal. It would be erroneous, of course, to lay the blame for this entire development on the Reformers alone, particularly since at points they sensed the problem and were prevented by factors beyond their control from taking appropriate action.

It must be recognized, however, that despite the failure of the Reform to free the church from cultural assimilation, it was by its very nature far more adaptable to the modern world than Catholicism could ever be. Indeed its basic flaws dare not close our eyes to its tremendous service to modern man. It has been the spiritual home of countless millions in many generations who could never have accepted the claims of Catholicism, and has been marked by a spontaneous and genuine piety rarely achieved by the latter. But its real vitality owes largely to subsequent developments such as Pietism and the English revivalist and free church movement, made possible, however, because the control of Catholicism was broken in the sixteenth century. Nevertheless Protestantism's confused and ambiguous social philosophy and social ethic, its divorce of objective justification from subjective transformation, and the absence of a central authority which alone can maintain a system of inclusive totality, made it particularly vulnerable to the ravages of humanism. Protestant professors and clergymen were often in the front ranks of the prophets of humanism, sawing off the very limb on which the Reformation rested, while Catholicism at least maintained a state of tension with "modernism" and "liberalism," particularly since the publication of the papal "Syllabus" of modern errors in 1864. But precisely this adaptability to the total society was another form of the erroneous attitude of the *corpus christianum* and has become the Nemesis of Protestantism. Since its attitude toward the world was assimilative rather than prophetic, "responsible" rather than catalytic, it too became imbedded in all the incongruities of the *status quo*. If we inquire then as to the spiritual blessings of Protestantism, we can say they were tremendous, but if we inquire, as in this paper, as to its degree of basic Christian restitution, we are driven to the dismal conclusion that it simply failed, at least in its original form, to sense the fatal social error of Catholicism and to effect an essentially renewed approach. In this analysis we are therefore justified in subsuming it under the contribution of medieval Christianity in as far as it remained "orthodox" and under that of humanism in as far as it was secularized.

V

The crisis of the mid-twentieth century, if this analysis is correct, is then to be sought in the realm of metaphysics. The theistic worldview which from the Constantinian period forward had provided the subsoil of western culture was challenged by the fifteenth-century Renaissance and received its first shattering blow in the French Revolution. From this blow it has never fully recovered but has had to give way increasingly to essentially immanentistic worldviews of humanism, which held out the hope of human fulfillment through the impulsion of innate energy. Today the humanist dream has in turn likewise defaulted, and has demonstrated unmistakably that it had rested on false premises. This failure or rejection of both the spiritual premises of Western civilization constitutes the crisis of our time. To be sure, powerful remnants of both views remain and will be influential in time to come. Indeed it would be most difficult to reduce all Western thought into one category or the other in any clear-cut fashion. This essay is merely an attempt to find something of a dominant characteristic in the subconscious presupposition of our time and is not directly concerned with the formal philosophies themselves.

Is the West, then, in a state of decline? If we accept the ideal either of medieval Christianity or of humanism, it seems that our answer must be a gloomy yes. Even if we accept neither, we are driven to the conclusion that the collapse of both the transcendentalist and the immanentistic value systems threatens to pull down the whole civilization with them. The West has lost the cohesive which holds the parts together to construct a meaningful whole. She is like a monster from whom the soul has departed but whose body continues to flail about in madness. The American reaction to the (Russian) Communist challenge is the reaction (e.g., "McCarthyism") of a people uncertain of its own faith. It is the reaction of a culture which can return neither to the theism which gave it birth, nor yet to the humanism which nursed it to maturity. Consequently modern man is not in the dilemma of two undesirable possibilities but simply at a dead end. There is of course a political dilemma between East and West, but the struggle between the communist and the western systems is mostly an echo, an Indian summer, of the two worldviews we have just described, the West of the transcendentistic medieval (in as far as she claims to be Christian), and the East (in so far as it is Marxist) of the immanentistic modern. But the masses, even when forced to choose one or the other of these two ideologies, sense instinctively the hollowness of both claims. In any event, Western culture today needs a new metaphysics, which it has not yet found. How and whether a new foundation for our present civilization will be found would be hazardous to predict. Humanly speaking, greater violence than what we have yet experienced seems inevitable, particularly because of similar upheavals of even greater proportions in the Orient. The prospect of a life and death struggle between closed cultural systems as the present alignment of East and West seems to predict is ample cause for men's hearts to fear.

VI

To characterize our time only in terms of "decline" would be to commit anew the errors of the *corpus christianum* and of humanism. More than this, it would be the sin of unbelieving pessimism, of the faithless steward who buried his talent in a napkin, for the crisis of our day demonstrates once more that the justice of God is tempered with mercy, that out of the marred clay He fashions new vessels. For the collapse of these two great systems of semi-truths will enable men to shift their point of departure from within the natural community to within the (gathered) religious community, to see more clearly than perhaps at any time since the Constantinian compromise that God works redemptively among men by way of the leaven, by the gathering of those who respond to His regenerative overtures, and that the incongruities of human existence and of the social order can reach final solution only as the regenerative process comes to maturity eschatologically. The impossibility of identifying the Christian community with any natural community or culture is being sensed increasingly, and scholars as G. J. Heering and Herbert Butterfield from various viewpoints are beginning to interpret the facts of Christian history accordingly.

It will be helpful to examine a bit more closely the "decline" of the West in this light. In the first place, it has shattered the myths of inherent progress. While it would be premature to speak of a popular revival, to reckon with transcendent reality is no longer the mark of naivety or bigotry. In the second place, the "decline" of the West and the emergence of the Orient have broken the monopoly which the West has exercised over Christianity for centuries. The failure of the church to domesticate the whole of Western culture has forced even the "Volkskirche," the mass or established churches, to become at least to a degree, gathered communities. Hence the West is no longer synonymous with Christianity. Meanwhile the new Christian communities of the Orient have developed a genius of their own and are exercising an increasing influence in the world church. This was brought home to the West with great forcefulness by the presence of the large numbers of Orientals at the ecumenical conferences at Oslo (youth) in 1947 and at Amsterdam in 1948. The Anglican bishop, Stephen C. Neill, reported, after a trip to Africa, that it is entirely within the realm of the possible that native African Christians may yet share in a re-evangelization of the West. In short, these developments emphasize in a new way the universality of the church of Christ and her transcendence over particularist cultures and social groupings. In the third place, this cultural disentanglement of the church is ethically salutary. Humanly speaking, a widespread turn to pacifism is hardly in the offing, but nevertheless the incompatibility of war with the Christian ethic is being felt increasingly. The same might be said with regard to divisions in the church. In the fourth place, there are encouraging trends even culturally. In philosophy there is some revival of realism, despite the ascendancy of existentialism, which still belongs to the nominalist tradition. The failure of the scientific structure built on nominalist assumptions is bound to renew and increase the interest in realism. The upper reaches of scientific thought have likewise been profoundly shaken. The discovery that the absolute laws of the physical universe are after all only relative (see above), has led scientists to interpret "indeterminacy" as actually meaning "creativity." It was this discovery, a Greek chemistry professor told me recently, that enabled him to accept the doctrine of grace as a new intervention of God outside the "laws" of nature. More familiar to us is the development of neo-orthodoxy in theology. Its most important feature in this context is its rediscovery of the transcendence of God and of the corresponding inadequacy and dependence of man. While none of these developments alone are likely to turn the tide of the West, they might well become major contributory sources for a genuine renascence.

VII

This general analysis leads to several concrete suggestions as to the Christian course of action in the time ahead.

1. Viewing the "decline" from within the gathered Christian community rather than within the natural community of the *corpus christianum* or of humanism leads to the conclusion that the crisis of the West is to be sought in the dilution of Christianity itself rather than in the secularization of culture in general. The latter is only a consequence of the former. Jesus called the Christian "the salt of the earth." The non-Christian can know God only within the limits of natural theism. Greater insights come indirectly through his observation of those who know God supremely through revelation, in our own age, through the Christians. It is when God in Christ becomes discredited by the unworthiness of those who confess His name that the God in Nature no longer seems inexorable. When those who know Him no longer reveal an awareness that "it is a terrible thing to fall into the hands of the living God," those who don't know Him need not worry about getting acquainted with Him. Preaching in the new era must therefore be pre-eminently Christological and Christocentric. Hand in hand with a rediscovery of the church as a gathered community must go a deep consciousness of the distinction between God's work in the realm of providence and His work in the realm of redemption. The church dare not confuse pious sentiments arising from experiences of natural theism with a vital faith in Christ. Obviously it is not the Christian task to denounce or judge such experiences but only to promote the truth.

Furthermore, viewing the "decline" of the West from within the New Testament concept of the gathered community, one is led to the conclusion, as we have already noted, that since Constantine the time may never have been more opportune for the church to disentangle herself from worldly alliances. Under the totalitarian powers, earnest Christians have been driven to the catacombs. In the West the forces of secularism have become so powerful and the number of people outside the pale of the church so great that the church can no longer presume to speak for the whole in the sense of the Constantinian compromise. World events will thus drive many Christians and Christian groups to rediscover their true relationship to the world. Admittedly, the opposite seems true in America for the moment, where many see the world struggle developing between the two supposedly opposite forces of Christianity and Communism. This indeed is the great temptation of American and other Western Christians. Yet even this situation will not change the minority position of Christianity in the culture of the West and is at any rate offset by the emergence of vital Christian minorities in other world cultures.

2. Next to evangelism, the most urgent task within the Christian Church—even more urgent than the much more publicized effort for ecumenicity—is the re-articulation of the Christian social ethic, of the relationship of the Christian and the church to the social order. Indeed one might well ask whether that is not essentially the evangelistic task of the day, the proclamation of a Gospel which reunites in the true New Testament sense, faith and works. The Catholic Church has retained her mistaken medieval vision in that respect, except as tactical modifications have become necessary, and as we have seen, Protestantism has not developed an adequate and unique social ethic of its own. In theory the oldest of the free church groups should be uniquely fitted for such a task of witnessing. But we too have shared in the general decline of Christianity. And devoted as we are to embers of a past spiritual flame we have largely failed to discover with pneumatic and prophetic freshness the parallel issues in our own society. But what remains of the original fire should be harnessed to this task—rather than, to the neglect of their own genius, they should fight with the armor of Saul—to

promote an evangel which still derives from earlier compromises. Such an approach of course presupposes a readiness to undergo the pre-Constantinian church-world tension and conflict.

3. Apologetics should seek to employ the discoveries and developments of science to which we have referred rather than to re-fight the battles of an earlier liberalism that is on the wane. Evangelical Christianity, based as it is upon God's self-revealing and redemptive acts in history because of man's fallen state, has done too little to relate its message to God's original creative charge to man to "subdue the earth." Too often its defense against the onslaught of militant secularisms or atheisms is conducted from a pre-Copernican platform. The church seldom succeeds in combining her conservatism vis-à-vis the attacks of worldliness with a forward look in the things of time which must change. Too often her fight for the faith degenerates into a reactionary fight for the privileges of the social *status quo*. The major task of Christian apologetics today is thus the proclamation of the special revelation of God in Christ in all its radical finality, but in terms which recognize empiricism within the realm of nature as being implicit in the divine charge to man to "subdue the earth." But in such an attempt to fight an advance-guard battle in the proper understanding of empirical science, we will need to be on guard constantly lest we fall into a new form of the old error of making science the touchstone of revelation or the still older one of supposing that a mass revival could somehow redeem the entire social order of the present aeon.

4. It appears that particularly in Europe, and to some extent in America, the creative days of the Christian clerical caste and the institutional church are over. Even the real effectiveness of modern mass media of communication in the evangelistic effort seems to be diminishing. The Church of Christ is essentially a pneumatic fellowship that expresses itself concretely in the Christian brotherhood, there where the "two or three are gathered." This fellowship is a fellowship of persons and is thus by its very nature what sociologists call a "primary group." The church can never assume the "secondary" character of the depersonalized urban society. It therefore seems clear that evangelism will make real progress among the industrial masses, as well as among other de-Christianized groups

in our society, only if the church will regain the personal and mobile lay character which has characterized all her truly creative periods, above all, the first centuries of the Christian era. The emphasis must be shifted from the salaried professional and the huge Gothic sanctuary to the man-to-man evangel of the simple self-supporting believer who shares the struggle of the common man.

5. There needs to be a recovery of eschatological comprehension, not speculatively but "existentially." We need to understand anew the ways of God in history. True, men have failed, but even in the midst of that failure the kingdom of God is moving toward fulfillment. Excessive preoccupation with attempts to read the signs of the times regarding future events cannot but dim our understanding of the here and now. Unhealthy speculation about the eschatological calendar can even be a way to bury the talent He has given. On the other hand, we need desperately a recovery of genuine eschatological expectancy, of the secret of the true saints of all ages who have awaited the aeon to come because they were already in it and whose future was illuminated as much by their present possession as was their present experience by their hope of future glory. Only such a faith will fit us to walk among the prophets of a new day that shall dawn, if God will, after the night that is descending upon the West, or to walk among those whose raiment is washed white if the "decline" of the West should be a feature in the final act of the drama of history. Only thus can we say, "Whether we live therefore, or die, we are the Lord's" and, "Amen. Come, Lord Jesus!"

The Anabaptist Dissent
The Logic of the Place of the Disciple in Society

John Howard Yoder

This essay attempts, in the context of current ecumenical discussions of the church's responsibility in society, and with special reference to the problems involving the use of violence, to elaborate a doctrine of social responsibility logically consistent with the concept of discipleship as understood and interpreted within the Anabaptist-Mennonite tradition. Since in practice the attitude here outlined has left certain problems unsolved, the primary aim herein is not yet to advocate specific courses of action but rather to define principle consistently.

Discipleship is here understood as denoting a particular attitude toward the Christian life, whose major emphases are:

(a) That the Christian life is defined most basically in ethical terms. While forgiveness, membership in a social order, participation in worship, or receiving a revelation may all be very relevant factors, they do not rob *obedience in ethics* (*Nachfolge*) of primary rank.

(b) That valid ethical instructions are given in the New Testament, on the basis of which we may reliably know the precise content of the obedience which is expected of us. This attitude will be seen to contrast with other uses of the terms "obedience" and "discipleship" which are unrelated to precise ethical definitions, and which leave the content to be determined by a sort of enlightened opportunism.

The term "sect" may be used to translate this view of discipleship into the social framework. The term as here used should be clearly distinguished from its ecclesiological usage, where it signifies the separation of a church from other churches in order to be pure, as well as from its epistemological sense, where it refers to the claim to be sole possessor of the truth. "Sect" as here employed expresses a sociological phenomenon, a withdrawal from the "world" (i.e., from certain areas of social interaction) motivated by the desire to be obedient. These various sorts of sectarianism may sometimes coincide historically but such coincidence is not inevitable, and the social withdrawal here outlined does not equal either divisiveness or exclusiveness in matters of church teaching or church organization. The basic "dissent" of the sect as here spoken of is its refusal to assume responsibility for the moral structure of non-Christian society. Such a refusal correlates, both in logic and in history, with the otherworldly orientation and eschatological expectancy which the Anabaptists displayed. This view may be summed up by saying that the "sectarian," knowing that discipleship is a matter of individual calling and response, does not expect Christian ethics of the non-Christian.

I

The identification of the church with the whole of society, to which the "disciple" objects, is built into the foundations of Western social thinking. The realignment of church-society relations which took place in the epoch of Constantine has been called the "Fall of Christendom" for no little reason. Whether that realignment be approved or condemned, its importance cannot be denied, and its deepest meaning was in the resulting identity of church and society.

The establishment of Christianity as state-church, though symptomatic of this "fall," was not the most significant aspect of the change which took place. The church's accepting the tolerance and favor of the state was less serious than her willingness, on behalf of the state and in line with the interests of her own hierarchy, to make her membership identical with that of society and to serve as social cement, as guarantor of morale and cohesion for the social order of the day. That this sort of church-society bond can exist entirely without any established church is easily seen in American Protestantism, which, although jealously guarding its separation from the state, still insists on the Christianization of all society and feels authorized to dictate to society, including the state, what that Christianization will mean in detail (see, e.g., *The Christian Century*, whose name is not insignificant). The disrepute of the established-church setup in some parts of Europe thus does not by any means signify the abandonment of the Constantinian viewpoint as long as the church, even if deprived of its favored position, continues to think of her moral responsibility as englobing society *en bloc*.

Infant baptism is closely related to the church-society identification, as the Reformers knew when they decided to conserve this one element of Roman tradition; but this compromise is only a symbol of the deeper identity, axiomatic for Luther and Zwingli alike, of church and *Volk*. This identity was the occasion of the "Anabaptists" break with Zwingli, beginning in October, 1523, over the issue of the competence of the city council to determine matters of church reform, and not, as often interpreted, with the first baptism in January 1525. The "Anabaptists" never accepted this name as descriptive of their position, and modern European theologians' attacks on infant baptism (Barth, Leenhardt), staying as they do within Volks-church lines, in no way tend to vindicate the Anabaptists.

Much of what is characteristic of Western society results from the Constantinian liaison of church and world. The church by her acceptance of the system became, not an autonomous moral force representing in the midst of the world the demands of God's righteousness, but simply the moral backbone, the morale-giver, the sanctifier of the society she was tied to. When later society became divided into East and West, so did the church; when modern nations developed, the church again was divided, everywhere blessing the particular (and conflicting) political and military designs of their peoples, be they defensive or aggressive, altruistic or selfish. Such a situation as now bothers the ecumenical movement in its efforts to straddle the iron curtain is inevitable in view of the presuppositions shared by churches on both sides of the line. Thus it may come to pass that with the decline or collapse of the West will fall much that is Christian, proving that the church could not sanctify society and that she should not have tried. Christian missions are now discredited in some quarters as having been agents of Western imperialism. Though such may never have been the missionaries' motives, and though the danger is now clearly seen by mission strategists, such a result was hardly avoidable with the missioning churches as closely bound to their home cultures as they have been.

The church-society identification is a deeper matter than the differences between schools of theological thought. From orthodoxy to rationalism and the social gospel and back to neo-orthodoxy, the postulate of "responsibility" was never questioned, least of all in the contemporary neo-orthodox revival, which has provided great new impetus for political and social action in the direction of society's sanctification. The term "responsibility" may for the purposes of our discussion be taken as a label for the social-ethical position whose crasser form we called "Constantinian."

II

After sketching the attitude toward church-society relations which has characterized western Christendom since Constantine, we turn to a sharper analysis of the opposite position, which the advocates of responsibility call a sectarian or withdrawal strategy (John C. Bennett's term).

The Disciple, i.e., the Christian who sees his "Christian-ness" as being an ethical matter, would first of all insist that "responsibility" is ethically ambiguous, since its says nothing definite about either ends or means. What matters to him is obedience, and that in light of concrete demands of God upon him, not as a strategic choice of means to reach an end assumed good.

A strategy of responsibility must lead, by the very ambiguity of the criteria used, to ethical compromise which undermines the church's moral authority. The Constantinian church's assimilation of paganism, the medieval church's approval of the feudal order and use of the Inquisition, Luther's acquiescence to bigamy and willing use of German nationalism, Münzer's use of the sword to bring in the kingdom of God; all were instances of responsibility's replacing other ethical norms. Centuries of theology drawn from the Old Testament theocracy, from justification by faith, from Aristotle, or from the idea of the kingdom of God (anywhere but from New Testament ethics) have made the position of compromise respectable, and the epithets "irresponsible," "sectarian," have become as emotionally colored as "Schwärmer" or "Red." This doesn't make the compromise justifiable on New Testament grounds.

The issue between withdrawal and responsibility as social strategies comes to the sharpest focus in the area where the Anabaptist-Mennonite application of Christian nonresistance leads the Disciple into conflict with the demands of society through the state in matters concerning war and the police function of the state. Here the Mennonites, supporting themselves on the entire New Testament for their nonresistance and precisely on Romans 12–13 for its application to the state and to sin, have a very clear position (Schleitheim Art. VI); the state is ordained by God to bear the sword "outside the perfection of Christ," whereas the Christian "within the perfection of Christ" refuses to participate in any human scheme of vengeance. He leaves vengeance to God (Romans 12:19) who in turn uses the state as His servant (Romans 13:4). This analysis thus sees a clear dichotomy in God's dealing with evil; in the order of conservation, He uses the violent state to punish evil with evil to preserve a degree of order in society and leave room for His higher working in the order of redemption, through nonresistant self-giving love in Christians. Such a dichotomy is no novelty in Christian thought; what was new was the idea that the Christian should live *only* on the level of redemption. It is the contention of this paper that such a rigorous use of the dichotomous analysis, with the Christian's conscious obedience limited to the realm of redemption, and God's Providence working in the realm of conservation without the help of the Christian's compromising, throws a remarkable light on various aspects of the problem of Christian ethics in society.

III

We turn to several applications of dichotomy as a critical principle in ethics. The prime example is still the question of violence and war. As we have seen, the Mennonite view sees room in God's plan for both the violent state and the nonresistant church without thereby justifying the state's ethics as valid for Christians. The state churches, not respecting this dichotomy, see God as working through the violent church, error which takes away her redemptive nature; liberal pacifism, just as unaware of the dichotomy, envisages a nonresistant state, and is justly accused of underestimating man's sinfulness. Neither view is logically adequate or pragmatically constructive, precisely because of the un-Biblical presupposition of "responsibility" so defined as to hide the difference between God's two distinct ways of dealing with sin in society. On one hand the pacifist feels constrained to prove that if the whole nation were nonresistant, aggressors would somehow stay away and criminals be reformed; on the other hand the church uses crusades and the Inquisition to sanctify all of society.

The reality of sin in man and therefore in society is such that even those ethical systems which aim at responsibility were obliged to introduce a dichotomy somewhere within the system. The Catholic approach draws this line between the law, the minimum standard required of sinners, and the counsels, required only of monks and saints. Thus by having two contradictory ethical systems, casuistry winds up having really none. Luther puts the same line in another place, between the Christian as citizen, who must make war, and the Christian as neighbor (the same man, however) who should return good for evil. This two-realm theory combines with an anti-ethical interpretation of justification by faith to permit the continued participation of the Christian on both levels of ethics, because he's only a poor sinner anyway. Both the Catholic and the Lutheran views thus recognize the essential impossibility of one ethical system for both Christians and non-Christians, but by failing to put the line where it belongs, i.e., between the church and the world, they force the dualism *into* Christian ethics, thus making grace cheap, and sacrificing the normative character of the love ethic. If, in the first place, the church had not been identified with society, the error would have been much more easily recognized and avoided.

Calvin, on the other hand, refused to admit the dichotomy so easily into his ethics, attempting by discipline of church and of state to make everyone live like a Christian. One result of this effort was the need to use the Old Testament rather than the New as an ethical guide for the new theocracy; another was the growth of Puritanism, which drove the dichotomy still further within the individual by imposing external ethical conformity on everyone (see on this point psychoanalysis's view of the great importance of purely external ethical sanctions of the origin of personality disorders). Puritanism may be given much of the credit for what is valuable in Anglo-Saxon civilization, particularly with relation to the order of conservation, but its general tone can hardly be called redemptive, and its ethics became generally more stoic or pharisaic than Christian.

In contrast to liberal pacifism, the dichotomist analysis attributes real value in God's plan to the "good heathen" (term used by J. A. Liechty) on the level of conservation, who through honest application of sub-Christian ethics do carry a real responsibility for justice in the social order. The Bible's injunctions to support the government and to pray for it, as well as the repeated statement of the state's function, all indicate that in this framework some morality is better than none. But what the Anabaptist-Mennonite dichotomist challenges is the validity of that *kind* of goodness on the redemptive level of Christian ethics. The sword, wrote Sattler at Schleitheim, is ordained of God, but outside the perfection of Christ. Thus while disagreeing with liberal absolutism as to the real value of the services of an Eisenhower or a Hershey (to use men of Mennonite origin as examples), the dichotomist disagrees equally with the "responsible" view that since they are ministers of God (Romans 13:4), they are therefore also applying New Testament ethics the way God wants Christians to.

IV

This development has built upon the question of nonresistance an attitude to the state and thus to society. It may rightly be asked whether this attitude is supported by other New Testament teachings than that on nonresistance. The thesis that God works in the world on two separate levels, one through the conscious obedience of Christians, the other by ruling over and balancing against each other men's disobediences, requires Biblical confirmation. Aside from the orthodox doctrine of providence, which says also that God uses "all things" for good, and in which the conscious obedience of Christians may be distinguished from the blind obedience of heathen nations or of the forces of nature, the most direct treatment of this question is probably that given by the New Testament within the framework of its eschatology. In the end-time which stretches from the ascension of Christ to His return, there seem, according to the New Testament, to be two related but distinguishable agents of God's working in the world (see esp. O. Cullmann, *Reign of Christ and Church in the New Testament*). Both are, each in its own way, precursory forms of the kingdom of God, which in its fullness shall be realized only at the end of the present era. Both are results of the work of Christ, and both are necessary in God's final triumph. The kingdom of the Son begins with the elevation of Christ to the Father's right hand, extension of the triumph already begun in His resurrection over the "authorities, dominions, principalities, powers" which semi-symbolically represent the demonic cohesions and autonomous structures of the present social order. This triumph, whose ultimate certainty is already sealed, will be complete when the Son turns over the kingdom to the Father after the destruction of the last enemy.

This rule of Christ thus involves present time, our own human history included, and its extent is that of all creation. The body of Christ, on the other hand, is composed of those who have been chosen, called, and regenerated, and who carry out in the world the redemptive work of Christ, as ministers of reconciliation. As member of the body, a Christian is related to his Head by a much closer bond than that which relates the subjects of the Kingdom of the Son to their King. Both the Christian and the "principalities and powers" are subject to Christ, but in entirely different ways. The kingdom of Christ and His body are thus distinct entities with distinct functions in God's plan. If this reading of Pauline eschatology is accurate, it would be possible, entirely apart from the precise issue of nonresistance and the state, to justify biblically the clear separation of the Christian's ethical function in the world from other functions which though recognized to be necessary and used of God, are not the Christian's particular assignment.

Certain ethical conclusions may in this case be drawn from the apostle's teaching about our "end-time" situation. Neither the Lordship of Christ nor the kingdom of God is a sufficiently precise concept to serve as a base for a Christian ethics. The kingdom of God, because its eschatological fulfillment will efface the present difference between church and world and will destroy the particular time-bound necessity for the peculiar redemptive, cross-bearing, and witnessing mission of the body of Christ. The Lordship of Christ, because the term is ambiguous, not distinguishing between the two ways that Lordship is now expressed.

Because the work of the church is what gives real meaning to history, we need not be ashamed of our "irresponsibility" in giving our attention as Christians to the church's particular tasks, and thus leaving to the "good heathen" the functions, necessary but non-redemptive, which fail to accord with our particular mission. The ultimate triumph of Christ as King over the "powers" is achieved not by the church's compromise with the already potentially defeated rebellious world order, but by her faithful execution of her own redemptive task. That this interpretation of the New Testament eschatology is watertight is not the contention of the present writing; but the exegetical possibility of such a confirmation of the dichotomous approach to society is not without significance.

V

The Anabaptist-Mennonite tradition, theologically understood, is seen to represent not simply a branch of Protestantism with a particular "talent," but a historical incarnation of an entirely different view of the Christian life, of the work and nature of the church, and fundamentally also of the meaning of redemption. A schematic comparison may help to render evident how completely the two systems, here called responsible and sectarian, are distinct all through their doctrine, in a way consistent with their differing views of society.

Central in the difference is our reaction to the presence of evil in the world. That there is evil, and that its existence requires a place in our thought, was questioned by the liberalism of a generation ago, but both history and theology have in recent years brought thinkers back to recognition of the real sinfulness of man's actions. The issue at stake between the sectarian and responsible positions is not whether our ethics shall take account of the sinfulness of man, but rather the way in which that cognizance will modify the ethics of love.

The responsible view is that, since we are responsible (this being an axiom), the presence of evil, in ourselves and in the world, removes the ethics of love from the realm of possibility, since we must use power, including physical violence if necessary, to restrain evil in the interest of a justice which, though not the kingdom of God (since we who would enforce it are also sinners), is relatively better than the wrong which would result (and for which we would be responsible) if we applied only nonresistant love. The love norm in ethics, while not utterly disqualified, is thus subordinated to the "realism" which reads the presence of sin as invincible in our aeon and therefore as requiring that we accommodate our ethical goals to the impossibility of love. The presence of sin thus itself becomes a second ethical norm beside that of love, and when two contradictory principles coexist, simple logic tells us that neither can remain a true norm. What results is a justification of relativism and opportunism, with no standards definable as valid for all, and with any compromise justified. And so it happens that "responsible" theologians, whether Catholic, Lutheran. Reformed, or neo-orthodox, are to be found on both sides of every major political division and every war, justifying with the same "realist" (i.e., opportunist) logic the adoption of utterly opposed lines of action. Thus the "responsible" ethic introduces the fact of sin in such a way as to destroy all the real validity of ethics itself, since if the same doctrinal framework supports contradictory conclusions it is useless as a guide for really knowing anything sure about the good.

The traditional liberal thought in ethics did fail, in large part, to take sin seriously enough, and thus did tend to see the adequate ethical fulfillment of the requirements of love as a simple possibility. This sort of perfectionism contradicts both history and Christian doctrine. There exists, however, in the sectarian approach, another type of perfectionism on an entirely different level. The Anabaptist who insisted on following the commands of the Master the way they seemed to be meant had no illusions about his own sinlessness, and no optimism as to obedience's being a simple historical possibility, even though he has sometimes been interpreted as if this had been the case; his real contention was on a different level. He refused to admit, as ethics must if it is to remain ethics, that an "is" makes an "ought." That the human male naturally has adulterous tendencies doesn't make adultery right, Mr. Kinsey's thesis to the contrary notwithstanding. Nor can the presence of sin become a new norm in ethics, which would justify lowering the goal to coincide with our accomplishments. Biblical realism means not making of the presence of sin an excuse for more sin; it means awareness that loving action will be costly and ineffective, and that the goal is never reached. Biblical perfectionism affirms not a simple possibility of achieving love in history, but a *crucial* possibility of participating in the victory of Christ over the effects of sin in the world. Obedience for the sectarian thus involves the cross, and the presence of sin has been worked into ethics, without either undermining the integrity of ethics as part of a valid theology or cheapening the work of redemption. This perfectionism of the cross is therefore not optimistic about either the world's or the Christian's goodness; it dares simply share the Bible's own confidence that with God all things are possible.

Grace means, in the context of responsibility ethics, purely forensic justification by faith. God is merciful, not only toward our unwitting sins and our daily missteps, but also toward the intentional compromises which we make in His name because we can't be perfect, the conscious disobedience dictated by our realism. And grace must have this meaning when one believes both that accomplishing His will is an absolute impossibility and that what He really wants is that we dilute His will to a level where it can be used to run society responsibly. Forgiveness as thus defined fits into the general repudiation of ethics which the presence of sin was used to justify, and the work of redemption centers at the cross.

As the cross becomes meaningful in the New Testament only in relation to the resurrection and to Pentecost, so in sectarian ethics is forgiving grace rightly understood only in the context of empowering grace. Interpreting justification by faith as a ratification for conscious compromise with the presence of sin is what Paul calls sinning "that grace may abound": what Bonhoeffer called "cheap grace." The Biblical perfectionist refuses to flatten God's goodness into mere forgiving mercy. He experiences redemption as a brand-new dimension of possibility for discipleship given the new man through his participation in the body of the risen Lord, and knowing the reality of this new life, he refuses to spiritualize or to eschatologize it out of the realm of his earthly living and doing. This also is the grace of God, that we may walk in newness of life.

We have traced the difference of ethical views backward, so to speak, into the differing concepts of grace which are presupposed; now we may look in the other direction, toward the application of general principles to specific problems. Here the sectarian believes that with the Holy Spirit's help, the congregation can deduce from the New Testament a set of instructions, commands, and prohibitions, which are objectively valid in that they translate the will of God adequately for all Christians at a given time and place. On the basis of these principles, just as binding for my brother as for me, church discipline is possible, and the church's unity has an ethical aspect, as being separate from the world and committed not only to piety, or to forgiveness, or to obeying the individual intuition, but to a definable, teachable, and disciplinable obedience. The Anabaptists who reached the "Brotherly Union" of 1527 listed church attendance, wine-houses, and the use of arms as the identifiable forms of separation from the world for their age and culture.

It would take us too far astray to discuss here the way in which the "responsible" church, consistently with its general attitude, refuses to define visibly its separation from the world, or to understand its unity as ethical and involving discipline. Our interest here is in the observation that opportunism in ethics, justified as we have been by the presence of sin, involves a denial of the validity of any such sort of objective instructions to make concrete the will of God. This denial takes several forms, chief of them being the charge of "legalism"; a charge which carries great emotional weight behind equally great conceptual ambiguity. Legalism can refer to the belief that by observing a set of rules, which in principle are within human possibilities, we will be just in the sight of God. This view is unscriptural and runs counter to what we know of the sin in even the Christian's heart. And this is furthermore not what the sectarian believes. The second use of "legalism" is in reference to the belief that it is possible, as a guide to discipleship and discipline, for Christians to know adequately what God demands of those who have received His grace; and this view involves neither optimism nor works-righteousness. It really amounts to nothing more than an affirmation of the possibility of a Christian ethic, of a valid ethical generalization. By using "legalism" as an epithet to cover two distinct positions and attach to one the reproach belonging to the other, the advocate of responsibility is freed from the danger of having to comply to any distinctively Biblical norms, and free to seek his ethics among extra-Biblical sources.

The general heading for these extraneous sources is "The Freedom of God." God is so free, according to the so-called Barthian theology, that He may contradict Himself and it would be impious for us in our ethics not to leave Him that liberty. He may call one Christian to war, to assassinate a tyrant, or to commit abortion, and another to refuse all participation in killing. The ways in which He gives this leading are several, and should be listed here, since this is really the heart of responsibility ethics, even though ethical theorists seldom analyze in detail what to them is axiomatic.

(a) Human solidarity, as an ethical postulate, means not primarily the unity of humanity, but rather the contrary, the ties man has with family or nation *as over against* the rest of mankind. He who is born Swiss is meant by God to be Swiss, and that includes defending the Swiss people against attack, i.e., loving the Swiss more than the Germans or the Russians. In spite of its altruistic tone, the word "solidarity" thus signifies in reality the crassest collective egoism, and it is argued that when God lets us be born into a nation, He thereby reveals that for us His will is that we identify ourselves with the egoism of that particular group.

(b) Since Luther, the term "vocation" has been the pivot of an ethical pun. Instead of meaning that one's occupation should correspond to God's call and thus literally be a "calling," the interpretation has been the opposite, that God's will must conform to my present occupation. If I am hangman, prince, soldier, or saloonkeeper, God wants me to be that, and be a good one; the rules for being a good hangman, etc., are derived not from the Gospel but from the autonomous standards already defined by the professions of hangmanship, statesmanship, barmanship, etc.

(c) Some ethical theorists admit honestly that, since love ethics are unattainable, our day-to-day compromises must be guided by elements drawn from pagan philosophies (Roman concepts of justice, Greek ideas of virtue). This approach has the merit of honesty.

(d) *Intuition* and *opportunism* are generally discredited terms, and few would admit their serving as ethical principles. Clear analysis, however, will demonstrate that a rejection of the love ethic as ultimately determinative really leaves nothing else to build on than situation (opportunism) or sentiment (intuitionism). Whether the label used be "pneumatic ethics," "prophetic vocation," "realism," or "responsibility," the fact remains that we have to do with an ethical decision derived elsewhere than from the sources of Christian ethics.

The above examples are representative, not exhaustive. They are intended only to demonstrate that nowhere, except in an honest espousal of paganism, does the use of extraneous ethical sources provide any element which is objectively verifiable and equally valid for all, which could be an adequate foundation for elaborating, teaching, and living a Christian ethics which is more than a rationalization of what a non-Christian would also do for the same reasons. It is thus in full consistency with its view of society and of grace that "responsible" ethics makes of Christianity a religion, not of redemption, but of preservation; a sanctification of the existing order which it reinforces with religious sanctions and assures of the unmerited mercy of God. The sectarian perfectionist has no objection to the existence of the present order, nor to the use of sub-Christian moral guides by those who are responsible for it; this he understands as belonging somehow in God's plan. What he objects to, on grounds of logic and honesty, is using the descriptive term "Christian" to refer to a system whose presuppositions are such that the distinctive ethical import of the Gospel is pragmatically declared irrelevant. But this usage is as old as Constantine and can hardly at this late date be dropped from the language.

VI

Contemporary theology has been greatly influenced by the contention of Schweitzer that all the ethical teaching of Jesus was derived from His expectation of a literally imminent end of the present world order. Some have therefore reasoned that since the end failed to come as expected, therefore the ethics of Jesus should be suspended or discarded. Without claiming any authority to deal with the exegetical questions involved in this view, we may be permitted to see in it two truths which situate New Testament ethics in God's plan without reference to calendar predictions.

(a) The ethical reasoning of the school following Schweitzer (see, e.g., Paul Ramsey, *Basic Christian Ethics*) takes the form of a hypothetical syllogism:

>Major: If the present world order subsists, we must be responsible for it.
>Minor: Jesus said, don't be responsible for it;
>Concl: Therefore Jesus thought it won't subsist.

The major premise is the presupposition of responsibility whose *Selbstverständlichkeit* this paper challenges. The minor is the result of a reading of the New Testament in which the sectarian could concur. That the conclusion drawn from the juxtaposition of an unexamined presupposition with a Biblical interpretation marked a milestone in the history of theology is not our concern here. We are interested only in indicating to what extent this reasoning rests upon and thus confirms the view that the ethic of Jesus shows little concern for the maintenance of the present order. And if this lack of concern was coupled with an expectation of a near end to world history, such a foreshortening could only serve to reinforce the impressions that Christians, who belong to the coming kingdom, have higher things to do than to attempt, by compromise and by accommodation to the presence of sin, to keep the moribund world order in decent running condition. The later epistles' cautiousness about setting dates involves no softening of this low evaluation of the non-Christian order.

(b) Much of what in the Gospels is eschatological prediction finds its fulfillment in the events between the crucifixion and Pentecost. Here too we can agree with those who emphasize how central in the teaching of Jesus were the events involving Himself and His destiny, as being the center of the fulfillment of God's plan. The coming of the kingdom can serve as a sanction for radical ethics either if it means an end to chronological history and a judgment, or if it means the coming of the Spirit to impart the power of the resurrection. That something new has come in Christ, namely, the power to become sons of God, is the sectarian's "realized eschatology" and his reason for refusing to lower his ethics to the level of pre-Christian historical possibilities. If really Christ's work brought into the world something so living and so new that the existing order is thereby revealed as moribund, then the length of time remaining before the ultimate judgment is irrelevant for ethics, but the confirmation that only the kingdom matters and that the sin in the dying system, having been conquered, is no reason for lowering our ethical sights is of real meaning in the dialogue about responsibility.

VII

The writer of these pages is convinced of the logical consistency of the "sectarian" view as here outlined, and of the fundamental ethical chaos involved in the compromises made in the interest of responsibility. This sectarian view corresponds closely with the New Testament teaching, and regains relevance in every period where a rediscovery of committed discipleship leads to persecution. It, however, appears that religious groups dedicated to this ideal have uniformly deformed or abandoned it with the passage of time, being apparently unprepared for toleration and for transmitting their vision to their children. This historical incapacity of the sectarian approach to maintain its immediacy calls for further study.

Hearken to me, you who pursue deliverance, you who seek the Lord; look to the rock from which you were hewn, and to the quarry from which you were digged. Look to Abraham your father. . . .

—Isaiah 51:1, 2

For no other foundation can anyone lay than that which is laid, which is Jesus Christ.

—I Corinthians 3:11

The triumphant Church, as has been said, does no more resemble the militant Church than a quadrangle resembles a circle, and established Christendom resembles it just as little. Nevertheless, the militant Church alone is the truth; the triumphant Church and established Christendom are vain conceits.

—Kierkegaard, *Training in Christianity*

VOLUME 2

1955

PREFACE by Paul Peachey

The quest for the Church is one of the perennial themes of Christian history. In our time this search has been rendered exceptionally difficult by the divided state of Christendom and the profound social and cultural upheavals of recent decades. Moral and religious problems have vastly outgrown traditional concepts of Christian faith and practice. Denominational structures present themselves ever more clearly as a distortion of the Gospel. To be sure, the spineless quality of what usually passes for ecumenicity-by-indifference may be even "less Christian" than denominational fervor. But if the supernatural redemptive reality of the Christian Church is again to break forth, if the "church" is to become the Church anew, it is clear that we must emerge from the strictures of dead traditions where we are bound by them. Indeed, a fresh attempt to study the New Testament, as well as the Old, without the "aid" of denominational spectacles leads one to feel that our real difficulty is not the new problems of our age but the old biases which we bring to the study of the Scriptures. The apostolic writers were convinced that they had received "all things that pertain unto life and godliness" (II Peter 1:3). Consequently the shoulder-shrugging dismissal or turning back to God of some of our knotty problems is hardly Biblical. The ecumenical stirrings of recent years have made some contributions to our understanding. It is clear that salvation lies, not in a compromise of sovereignty and peculiarities among denominational structures, nor in a kind of universal agreement on some minimal "essentials," nor yet in the individualizing of salvation which hopes to solve the problem of the Church by bypassing it. Renewal will come only if the corn of wheat is ready to fall into the ground and die. The Church of Christ will break forth anew if we are ready to receive her. This is the issue as we see it. Mennonites, just as Christians of any other denomination, must face certain problems peculiar to their own heritage. The following pages deal largely with the Mennonite problem when it comes to specifics, but we are persuaded that the reality of which we hope, there may also be glimpses that have universal appeal.

P. P.

The Church in the Old Testament

John W. Miller

The Church of the New Testament regarded itself as the continuation and heir of the true Israel. One might point to a number of New Testament Scriptures and especially to Galatians 6:16 where Paul actually calls the Church the "Israel of God" in order to demonstrate the truth of this statement, but the confirmation lies already in the word *ekklesia* which New Testament Christians spontaneously adopted as the standard designation for their unique fellowship. It is now generally agreed that the early Christians chose this word, not because of its use in non-Biblical Greek, where it is never the title of a religious group (George Johnston, *The Doctrine of the Church in the N.T.*, p. 35), but because of its use in the Greek Old Testament, where it always translates the Hebrew word *Qahal* (or a word of the same root), meaning "the assembly of the congregation of Israel." In the earliest passages of the O.T., as L. Rost has shown, the word *Qahal* is used especially to refer to the calling together of the religious community for war or counsel (cf. Gen. 49:6; Num. 22:4), and then later to refer to that people called into a covenant relation with God at Sinai (Deut. 5:22; 9:10; 10:4; 18:16). That is why it can also be used to refer to the worshiping community during the era of kings (cf. I Kings 8:14 ff.) and later. The *Qahal* or Church of the O.T. is therefore composed of those to whom belong the covenant and the promises. They are the peculiar people of God. It is thus the continuation and fulfillment of this claim that the early Christians asserted when they adopted the word *ekklesia* to describe themselves. They claimed to be nothing less than the continuation of the true people of the one living God.

It is this fact which forces us to begin in the O.T. if we desire to come to a true understanding of the nature of the Church. The records of the N.T. Church are after all very scant, and the time span for which we have any records at all is very short. In the O.T. however we can observe the Church living through centuries of time, and meeting a great variety of problems hardly touched on in the N. T. It is this which makes the O. T. in this as in other phases of Christian thinking instructive for those upon whom the end of the ages has come (I Cor. 10:11).

I

There are various ways in which we might approach this discussion of the Church in the O.T., but there is no substitute for an effort to comprehend our subject in its historical development. We cannot of course in this brief essay set forth a detailed description of that history, but we must attempt nevertheless an outline of it as we find it in the O.T.

The story of the Church in the O.T. begins substantially with Abra-ham. About this the records are unmistakably clear, whatever one might think concerning the relation of the election of Abraham and the election of the Hebrew nation in Egypt. With the background of the teeming nations and the great world civilizations clearly in view (Gen. 10:11), the O.T. nevertheless declares that it was not through the instrumentality of some great world power, or some superior race that God began to work His purposes in this world, but through the calling of a single man and his immediate family (Gen. 12:1 ff.). To this man God promised land, heritage, and divine blessing, and through this man God asserted that the burden of curse which lay heavy on the human race would be lifted. The condition, however, was a call to a life of wandering. Family, culture, land, everything that gives a person security and status in this world, must be left behind, and Abraham must wander out not knowing where he is going. In this call and the quiet obedient response of Abraham (12:4), the O.T. sees clearly that which belongs to the essence of the people of God in contrast to the world. It is not perfection, for later in the Genesis story we see with unbelieving eyes how even pagans lecture this pilgrim on proper morality (Gen. 12:18 f.; 20:9 f.).

Nor is it blood or race, for from the loins of Abraham many races spring (25:1–6), but only they who grasp that peculiar character of the God-man relation, only they who by holding to the promise and by looking and longing for its fulfillment are willing to wander in a land that is not theirs, belong finally to that small nucleus of 70 souls (Gen. 46:27; Ex. 1:5) which is preserved in the midst of the great Egyptian sea.

In Egypt the family grew miraculously (Ex. 1:7) into a nation, and so began a new phase in the history of the Church in the O.T. Those events by which God released this nation from bondage to a great world power and set her on her journey to the promised land proved to be a mighty confirmation in *deed* of that election which came to the patriarchs only in the form of the naked word of promise (H. Wheeler Robinson, *Inspiration and Revelation in the O.T.*, p. 151). The remembrance of these deeds confirmed by God's self-revelation as Lord in the Sinai covenant provided in the centuries to come the most substantial basis for the Israelitic Church, and we hear her prophets and poets again and again reverting back to this foundation. Here Israel although a nation was nevertheless constituted as a Church.

The tribal structure of Israel during the succeeding decades of the wilderness wanderings and the occupation of the land of Canaan was an expression of this self-consciousness. It has been shown that the organization of Israel into twelve tribes was not determined alone by the accident of the number of Jacob's sons. Rather this tribal structure arose out of a passion for theocracy, and has its parallels in religious-minded societies outside the stream of O.T. history (M. Noth, *Das System der zwölf Stämme Israels*). One may wonder whether the history recounted in the Book of Numbers is not a bit schematized, and yet still see in the careful organization of the tribes about the ark of the covenant the most vivid declaration of this truth (Num. 2). Here was a society whose one center was the "Presence" as given to them in the mysterious, luminous "glory" which dwelt by the grace of God in the darkness of the fragile tabernacle (Ex. 40:34). Here was a society which did not produce its leaders, or seek to stabilize its organization by establishing a dynasty, but which could only quietly receive its leaders as the divine charisma manifested itself (Num. 27:16ff. and Judges).

This subordination of the totality of life under the rule of the "Presence" is, as von Rad has shown (*Der Heilige Krieg im alten Israel* [*Holy War in Ancient Israel*]), nowhere more vividly seen, than in the manner in which this loose confederacy of Israelite tribes waged their wars. On into the era of occupation, Israel was able to bring in a remarkable way the problem of the enemy into the circle of the *pansakralität* [*pansacrality*] (as Buber has called it). During the entire period of the wilderness wanderings and on into the period of Judges in the land, she stubbornly refused to establish a professional army, and subdued her enemies not with the arm of flesh, but with strange sacramental marches, with pitchers and trumpets and resounding shouts of faith in the God whom they had learned to know in their first crisis as a "Man of War" (Ex. 15:3). Even the enemies came in time to recognize that Israel was no ordinary community, which could be annihilated by the customary military methods. One of the favorite stories in ancient Israel had to do with a fearful king and a specialist in curses, whom he had called in to do what he realized no armies could do: stop the onward march of Israel. In high humor the Bible relates how God took the pagan diviner and made a minister of God out of him for Israel's sake (Num. 22–24).

In the period of Samuel, however, a subtle shift in the character of Israel made itself felt. The Church of Judges is by no means a sinless Church. In many ways it is the darkest picture of the people of God which the O.T. shows us. Nevertheless the request on the part of the people for a king, who would lead them out of their loose, ineffective tribal ordering to a more stable kind of society, was greeted with deep foreboding by the most spiritual leader of this transition time, Samuel himself (I Sam. 8). And his fears were all too quickly realized when in the first crisis Saul revealed how far he and his people had come from the ancient charismatic principles that governed the life of Israel in the wilderness, by refusing to submit to the fundamental conditions of Holy War (I Sam. 13, 15, cf. 15:15). It was indeed an authentic spiritual insight that even earlier prompted Gideon to refuse the proffered kingship and to point his people to the Kingship of God alone (Judg. 8:23).

The story of the Kings is the story of the degeneration of this primitive tribal community with its totally religious orientation into a secular state. The degeneration documented itself in numerous ways. Already, as indicated, in the reign of Saul, and then increasingly in the reigns of David and Solomon, emphasis was laid on the organization and equipment of a professional army. In other words, *the problem of the enemy was the first problem removed from the orbit of faith*. The chariot cities and the horses, the foreign pacts and the diplomatic niceties characteristic of the Solomon reign are the utter extreme from the Holy War as represented in Joshua and Judges. The centralization of the government in Jerusalem in combination with the loss of respect for the primitive tribal organization are further examples of the same process, and it would seem that the prophetic efforts that finally led to the division of the kingdom into two parts (I Kings 11:29ff.) were motivated by the hope that the people could be helped at least by that much to recapture their former simplicity under God. Along with all this of course came also the loss of the charismatic principle for selecting leadership. We see this principle still operating in the selection of Saul (I Sam. 10:1ff.) and again in the anointing of David (I Sam. 16), but the court intrigue that finally gave the kingdom into the hands of Solomon (I Kings 1) is potent witness to the completely secular viewpoint with which the people now approached the question of their king.

For a time the prophets sought to work with the Church that had become a state. We see especially in the activity of Elijah and Elisha the effort to tamper with the externalities of the Kingdom in the hope that the nation can once more be led back to its theocratic foundations. With the coming of the so-called writing prophets, however, this hope is given up. With them it is clear that the Kingdom of Israel is not the Church and must be judged (John Bright, *The Kingdom of God*, p. 67). In sharp opposition to the eschatology of their day which persisted in identifying the purposes of God with the structure of the body politic, Amos and those who follow must proclaim repeatedly a day of wrath and darkness.

Where then is the Church? Or in the gradual transformation of the primitive religious community into a secular state, have the purposes of God for mankind run dry? Although Amos spoke vaguely of the remnant of Joseph to whom God "perhaps" will show mercy (Amos 5:15), it was Isaiah who was given to see first and most clearly the place where the Church emerges in the midst of the ruins of his nation. After the famous rejection of King Ahaz and the complete frustration of all his efforts to persuade the nation as a body to accept the ways of God (Isa. 7:1–12), Isaiah receives an alternate plan. After he has pronounced openly and passionately the word of judgment upon the rejection of his age (Isa . 7:13—8:10), he is told to bind and seal his message of redemption in his disciples (Isa. 8:16). In other words he is to stand forth as a new charismatic leader and gather about him, like a father with his children (8:18), those who like Abraham are willing to step out from their homes and their cities and identify themselves with the lonely prophet. Together they are to learn what it means to disassociate themselves from the fears of their times and to trust in God alone (8:12f.). Together they are to meditate upon the secret hope of the Messianic child and the reign of righteousness and justice which He will bring. Then in the proper moment they are to step out and proclaim in the darkness where men wander about in utter confusion cursing their God and their king (8:19ff.) the advent of the Messianic age (9:1–7). A contemporary of Isaiah envisioned this same remnant gathered about its Adamic leader functioning in the societies of the world like gentle dew, watering and fructifying, and like a fierce lion, judging and destroying, until in the purposes of God the instruments of man's carnality and hatred are destroyed and the universal reign of peace has come (Mic. 5:7ff.).

Although the use of the word "remnant" as a terminus technicus has its own peculiar history, nevertheless the "remnant" question in the broader sense as it is posed particularly by Isaiah looms large in the remainder of O.T. history. Who belongs to the remnant? Each of the succeeding prophets must answer this question for their time. Jeremiah says: Not that confident throng which mills about in the temple courts shouting, "the temple of the Lord, the temple of the Lord, the temple of the Lord" is this (7:4), but only those who turn their back on Jerusalem and flee naked and helpless to the side of the enemy (21:8ff.), only those who in Babylon accept their banishment as the judgment of God and setting their hopes in God alone abandon all desires for an easy return to the bulwarks of Jerusalem (Jer. 29). Ezekiel says: Not those who vainly call Abraham their father (33:24), but those who submit to the easy yoke which God lays upon them in His gentle commands concerning the poor and the unclean (Ch. 18), and thus pass under the humbling outstretched bar (20:37). Such, say Jeremiah and Ezekiel, shall one day return to the promised land. To such God will give a new heart (Ezek. 11:19; 36:26) whereon are written the commands of God, so that all shall know Him from the least to the greatest (Jer. 31:3ff.). Over such will reign a prince of David from their midst (Ezek. 34:23f.; 37:22ff.; Jer. 30:21), and the center of their corporate life will concentrate once more as in the time of their primitive tribal fellowship in the place of God's presence: the "Glory" which dwells in the Temple holy of holies (Ezek. 43:1–5).

The little group that returned from Exile under Zerubbabel in 538 did not, however, experience the fulfillment of these prophecies, nor did they experience them when later Ezra and Nehemiah came to them with law book and reform program in hand. It was under this strain of a delayed parousia that the post-exilic Church of the O.T. had to live and work, and under this strain the spirits were discerned. The post-exilic prophets, in themselves evidence of the delayed fulfillment, summoned the people repeatedly to persist in their remnant calling and to put aside the unbelief that arose from the delayed Endtime. That however even among that small community of the Return in Palestine a further sifting had to take place, that again the Church and community were not one, is clearly indicated in Malachi, where we hear tired voices saying, "It is vain to serve God" (3:14). Here again it is only those who "fear" God (3:16), only those who in spite of all appearances continue to cling to God's promises in expectation of the coming Day of the Lord, whose names are written in the Book of Remembrance (3:16). Those who persist in "looking for the redemption of Jerusalem" (Luke 2:38) will *and do* greet the Lord when He comes (Luke 2:25ff.).

II

In the above survey many themes that would belong to a full treatment of the Church in the O.T. have been omitted or only lightly hinted at, but perhaps enough has been included to point up several crucial characteristics of the people of God as set forth there. We may discern by and large three contexts in which the Church of the O.T. was called upon to define her existence. The first was the Patriarchal period, when it became manifest that inclusion in the people of God was something other than a matter of blood and race. The second was the period of statehood when it became clear that the people of God was something other than a geographical reality. The third was the period of post-exilic Judaism when it became clear that the remnant of God was again something other than a well-regulated community of law. What the "something other" was in each case might be variously interpreted, but it always involved at least the following: (1) A forthright denial of the "appearances" of history which "seem" to controvert the walk of faith and a bold "nevertheless" (*trotzdem*) (Heb. 11); (2) A positive commitment into the hands of God, usually expressed through submission to the easy yoke of God's covenant law (e.g., Ezek. 18; Jer. 7:5ff.); (3) A persistent hungering and thirsting for the manifestation of God's reign in the near future. Again it bears repeating that it is Abraham, who wanders out from his home with no credentials but a command ringing in his ears and who lives out his days traversing a land that is his only by promise, who best embodies all three and thus provides the most vivid example of what it means to belong to the people of God. Particularly in him the Church of the O.T. challenges the Church of the N.T. as to whether the faith to which it calls men is a true faith.

A people so constituted reveals its nature further by the problems it faces. In the above survey two such problems stand out: the problem of leadership and the problem of the enemy. They are in reality one problem, for they are both involved in the more fundamental question of existence. How can a Church so constituted maintain its existence in the midst of an antagonistic world? How can it accomplish its ends, especially when those ends are worldwide? We have seen that the Church in the O.T. is only then truly the Church when both the question of the enemy and the question of leadership are left strictly in the hands of God. We have seen that it was precisely at that point where the sacrament of Holy War was arbitrarily manipulated and then substituted by a professional army that the disintegration of the Church into a state first expressed itself. We have seen too that the substitution of dynastic leadership for charismatic leadership belongs to the same process of disintegration. Therefore the Church of the O.T. challenges the Church of the N.T. particularly as to whether it is really committing the problem of the enemy and the problem of its own leadership into the hands of God alone.

Any study of the Church in the O.T. calls us finally as a N.T. Church to a re-examination of our foundation, whether it is broad enough and deep enough, and to a re-examination of the superstructure we are building whether it is appropriate to the foundation. The Church of the O.T. was gathered about the ruling "Presence," that is, its foundation, and its entire life was but an expression of that all-encompassing "Presence, " that determined the character of its superstructure. A study of the Church in the O.T. thus serves to underscore the importance of the two or three gathered together in the binding and loosing "Presence" of Jesus Christ (Matt. 18:15–20) as the ultimate reality and mystery of our existence.

III

Our study thus far will remain to a certain extent academic if we do not make at least some attempt to ascertain in how far the Church of the twentieth century is meeting the challenge posed for her by the Church in the O.T. What we say here must be necessarily provisional and inadequate. The contemporary Church is now a worldwide phenomenon, and all of us are extremely limited in our knowledge and judgment of even those parts of it with which we are most familiar. In spite of these limitations, it is necessary that we seek to examine ourselves in the light of the Biblical mirror.

Perhaps the most obvious failure in the contemporary Church, when measured by the above-mentioned threefold characterization of the Abrahamic saint, is the absence of any real "hungering and thirsting" for the manifestation of God's reign in the near future. This remains true even after Evanston where the theme of Christian hope held the theological center of attention. It remains true, because more than a highly publicized theological discussion is needed to overcome the extremely "this world" orientation of Western Christendom. While most Christians continue to speak of Jesus *Christ* and thus acknowledge their belief in a personal Messiah, they have largely lost the Messianic vision which impelled the early Church to pray repeatedly, "Come, O Lord Jesus!" (See Lev Gillet, *Communion in the Messiah*). It is of course true that doctrinal affirmations concerning a second coming occupy a prominent place in many Church creedal statements, but neither they nor fruitless millennial calculations are substitutes for the living expectancy of a new heaven and a new earth where righteousness dwells, which is the passion of Old and New Testament saints.

An even more obvious discrepancy between large segments of the contemporary Church and the Church of the O.T. exists in the area of leadership and enemy relations. If the history of the O.T. Church documents anything, it is, as we have seen, the importance of giving way to God's sovereign Spirit in the matters of leadership and the enemy. And yet it is precisely at these points that the Church again and again has become blind. Repeatedly when threatened by some danger from without or within she attempts to secure herself, either by setting up massive machinery for establishing at least the semblance of continuity and strength, or by identifying herself with the cultural and political forces that surround her, thus accepting both the world's attitude and approach to the enemy. For the Church in the United States, for example, there is no more disturbing fact than the widespread acceptance by "Christian" people of the militaristic institutions as both necessary and right. Measured by the prophetic witness in the O.T. Church, such Christians bear the name falsely (cf. Isa. 7:9). A Church that does not trust God for its existence even in the face of the destroying enemy, but relies on the arm of flesh is, according to the standards of the Church in both Old and New Testaments, no Church of the one true God who is the Father of Jesus Christ. It is this fact which makes ecumenical fellowship profoundly problematic for the so-called "Peace" Churches. The question is not one of isolated dogmas, but of the whole character of faith by which the Church lives. At the same time, however, the "Peace" Churches must remember that a correlative of their attitude toward the enemy must be the submissive way in which they receive their leadership. A "Peace" Church that organizes itself in an autonomous, self-sufficient way and seeks either by hierarchical or perchance democratic machinery to secure its leadership is contradicting itself. The faith that trusts God for the problem of the enemy also trusts God for the gift of charismatic leadership necessary for every need.

Whether the contemporary Church is living in the expectancy and realization of the repeated miracle of the binding and loosing "Presence" of God in its gathered fellowship is impossible to say. Certainly in many cases the Church has settled for something less. The multiplication of large, unwieldy congregations, the ever-resurgent cult of the popular preacher, the almost universally accepted practice of concentrating in the hands of a few the responsibility for exercising spiritual gifts have often tended to make the Sunday morning gatherings of the Church pious theatricals, where nothing more is expected than a little entertainment, a little peace of mind, and perhaps a little challenge to nobler living. There are all too few Sunday morning gatherings of the Church about which an outsider would spontaneously exclaim, "God is really among you" (I Cor. 14:25). It is perhaps this defect at the core of her worship experience that more than anything else vitiates the testimony and effectiveness of the Church in today's world. It is not simply a rhetorical conclusion to say that if we fail here, we cannot really succeed at any other point.

Spirit and Form in the Church of Christ

Paul Peachey

The foregoing essay has placed the Christian Church in the larger setting of the people of God. It has made clear that from the start the people of God has been spiritually constituted (cf. Gal. 3). Abraham's response to the call of God was an act of faith which had nothing to do with human institutions. But the formation of the people of God already from the outset assumed also an ethnic form. It became a body united by bonds of blood, tongue, culture, and territory. Adherence to the people of God in the outward sense, therefore, did not guarantee for each member the spiritual commitment upon which this people was constituted (in Abraham). Thus the spiritual reality was in constant jeopardy. This obscuring of the spiritual dimension was one of the roots of the recurrent apostasy which characterized Jewish history. But the epistle to the Galatians makes it clear that the constitutive reality of the Old Testament people of God is to be sought, not in the Mosaic legal structure, but in the spiritual community of faith established in Abraham.

The people of God as an ethnic community was to perform, however, an important function in redemptive history. Incorporated into the Mosaic economy which was designed as a schoolmaster to lead to Christ (Gal. 3:24), the people of God, now often more ethnic than spiritual, prepared men to understand the selective process of redemption. Israel redeemed from Egypt symbolized the spiritual deliverance of the faithful and prefigured the people of God to be assembled in Christ.

But as Miller makes abundantly clear, the ethnic community as such could never indeed be the people of God. For not only did the ethnic obscure the spiritual, but it led to constant confusion between the visible ethnic and institutional structure and the underlying spiritual reality. The people of God, ethnically conceived, was thus foredoomed to failure. When finally the Israelitic cup of apostasy was full, and then a humbled remnant returned to reconstitute the ethnic, but again with only limited success, the realization emerged ever more clearly that the people of God is a spiritual reality and must be spiritually constituted, i.e., by the response of faith.

With this realization we come to the New Testament. The spiritual essence of the people of God is intimated in Christ's initial message: "The time is fulfilled, and the kingdom of God is at hand; repent, and believe in the gospel" (Mark 1:15). Again and again these words appear on the lips of Jesus. It is a spiritual reality which He has come to communicate. But again and again the disciples, traditional Jews that they were, linked the idea of the kingdom of God with their national ethnic past. In this they thought as did the Pharisees who inquired, "when the kingdom of God was coming," and received the answer, ". . . behold, the kingdom of God is in the midst of you" (Luke 17:20f.). This kingdom-yearning of the disciples survived the resurrection—indeed, was revived by it, because at His death their hopes had been shattered. "We had hoped that he was the one to redeem Israel" (Luke 24:21)—and so at the moment of the ascension they still inquire, "Lord, will you at this time restore the kingdom to Israel?" (Acts 1:6).

We do not know what else transpired on the mount of ascension. The record tells only of the answer in which the apostles are told to wait for the power of the Holy Spirit. They had already been told of that event, but clearly they had not understood. They could not. They had been told, too, of the new fellowship, the *ekklesia*. To be sure, Christ had scarcely used the term, but everywhere it lies in the background of His message. But nowhere does He speak in terms that could be objectified or concretized into visible ethnic structures. It is the kingdom of God which He proclaims, the Spirit which "dwells with you" and shall be "in you" (John 14:17). And the contrast between the "among-you" (the disciples) and the non-disciples, is constantly sharply drawn (Matt. 5:46 ff.; 6:42 f.; Luke 22:25f.; etc.). This deep spiritual reality, however, they could not grasp (John 16:12), and as Paul was later to point out, cannot under any circumstances be grasped by the natural or unspiritual man (I Cor. 2:14).

It is therefore clear that Pentecost is truly the watershed in the redemptive history of the people of God. Here the reality of the spiritual kingdom of God breaks in power upon men. In Christian symbolism, Pentecost is Babel in reverse; it is the restoration of unity destroyed by Babel. Pentecost is the fulfillment of the coming of the Spirit which the prophets could only foresee in the distance (Joel 2:28–32; Acts 2:16). It is the spiritualization of the law, foretold by the prophets, when that which was expressed visibly in tables of stone, indeed in the whole sacerdotal, legal, and ethnic structure, would be engraved in hearts "of flesh" that would replace the old "stony heart" (Ezek. 11:19; Jer. 31:31–34; Heb. 8:8–13). That which was formerly symbolized in an external and visible order would now become an inner reality.

The distinction between the former and the latter state was not merely or primarily theological. It was a new reality. The coming of the Spirit transformed men in the center of their being. This transformation was an individual reality, as for example in the experience of Paul on the Damascus road. But at the same time it was a corporate or collective reality, as is most clearly seen in the day of Pentecost itself. The reality of the Spirit in the individual was the essence in which all the fellow believers participated, and so the immediate result of the outpouring of the Spirit was the *koinonia*, the fellowship, of Acts 2:42, a common participation that was so profound and inclusive that it transformed the attitude of the participants toward all of life's experiences and pursuits (ibid., v. 44f.; Ch. 4:32). This sharing, however, was a fruit and not the constitutive fact of the fellowship. The believers were "of one heart and soul," and hence their readiness to share.

The constitutive fact, on the divine side, of the people of God, is thus the Spirit, and on the human, the response of obedient faith. The fellowship of the saints is a spiritual reality. The Acts of the Apostles refers to the new Christian gathering of the people of God in a number of terms. The adherents are disciples (9:26; 20:7, etc.), brethren (11:29; 15:23, etc.), Christians (11:26), saints (9:13, 41), people for his name (15:14), and a multitude, congregation, or company (4:32; 6:5; 15:30, RSV). The most common designation, however, is *ekklesia*, a term which refers in the singular to the totality of Christians in one place or the universal people of God (5:11; 9:31, RSV), or in the plural, to local assemblies (15:41; 16:5), a term already used in the Septuagint for certain Old Testament assemblies, and in Greek political life for political assemblies (cf. Acts (19:32—Gr. *ekklesia*).

Whatever the designation, the attention is drawn to the inner reality rather than to a given form. The emphasis is on the gathering, not primarily on the calling out. What makes the church the church is not an organization or a ceremony but the fact of Christ's presence through the Spirit. This is constantly underscored, as it were, by the variety of circumstances under which the church comes to expression. Wherever brethren were to be found or wherever the brethren came together there was the church (21:4, 7). They could meet in public concourse or in private homes, though it appears that the breaking of bread was associated with the smaller group (2:46; 20:20). But always it takes Christ, through the Spirit, and the brethren as disciples, even as few as two or three (Matt. 18:20), to make the Church.

The "visible" or objective point of reference seems to have been, according to the earliest expression, "the apostles' teaching and fellowship, . . . the breaking of bread and the prayers." The significance of the apostles' teaching is everywhere largely writ in the Acts and anticipated in the Gospels. The apostles were designated as eyewitness to the words and work of Christ as it culminated in the resurrection. As such, they played a unique (onetime) role in the establishment of the church and then committed that witness to writing (cf. II Pet. 1:15, as a possible anticipation of the Gospel of Mark). These manifestations are not the Church, however, in a sacramental sense, but are rather visible expressions of the *koinonia* or fellowship. It is thus clear that while the essence of the church is the common participation of the disciples in the Spirit, yet this common participation means the gathering or assembling of a people, in accordance with the apostolic witness, who engage in fellowship, in prayer, and in the Lord's Supper.

The Church Visible and Invisible

The fact that the spiritual reality of the people of God nonetheless finds visible expression leads us to the heart of the historic problem of the church, and of the contemporary controversy over the church. Where or what is the church? Is she spiritual or institutional? Is she visible or invisible? Is she an objective social structure or only an object of faith? Is she an objective entity in time and space or only a subjective experience, so far as her earthly expression is concerned? Above all, how is she constituted and where is she to be found among all the sects of Christendom?

These questions can be seen more clearly by a comparison of the three views of the church as most commonly advanced in contemporary discussions.

(1) The Catholic view. "The strict theological definition of the Church according to the New Testament is that it is the society of the faithful united by a complete confession of the same Christian faith, by the same Sacraments, and by submission to the same supernatural authority of the Roman Pontiff who is the Vicar of Jesus Christ" (*Dictionnaire de theologie catholique*, IV, 2110. Quoted by R. Newton Flew, *The Nature of the Church*, p. 17). As interpreted by Flew, this means that "the special characteristics of the Church are thus to be found in the wholly supernatural nature of its end and purpose, the special nature of the authority with which it is endowed, and the supernatural path of faith which its members are called upon to tread" (ibid., 18).

(2) At the other extreme of the spectrum is the Baptist view, also approximated by such groups as the Disciples and the Congregationalists, which asserts that the church is "a voluntary society for carrying on the work of Christ." "The organized Church as an institution is not for Baptists primary but secondary, functional and instrumental." ". . . The continuity of the true Church of Christ is maintained by the continuous working of the Holy Spirit through the agencies of the Gospel. . . ." "The distinctive contribution of Baptists to 'the Church Universal' is to be found in their insistence on the individual soul in relation to God, without human mediation of parent, priest, church, or sacrament, and in the conception of the entire ecclesiastical autonomy of the church. . . . They believe that the entire Gospel and programme of God in human history are based on the conception that God intends the individual to be the unit in his relation to mankind and deals immediately with every soul" (W. O. Carver in *The Nature of the Church*, 293, 289, 295, 297).

(3) Between these two extremes lies almost an infinite variety of views tending more toward the one or the other. The typical Protestant view occupies the middle ground. The objective and visible continuity of the church is stressed, but is to be sought, not ultimately in the *structure*, the supernatural authority of the "Vicar of Christ, "but in the *message*, in the word of God as proclaimed and in the right use of the sacraments. But the basic problem in any case is this: *Is the essentially supernatural fellowship, the people of God, embodied in or constituted by an historical organizational structure?* Is the organization of Christians or of Church government (potentially the papacy) identical with the church which is His body (Ephesians)? Can the organizational structure of any denomination, whether the Catholic hierarchy or the Mennonite conference, be called the church? Is the visible form essential or secondary? And is there a way out of denominational dividedness?

We have already noted the frequently stated antithesis of the spiritual versus the institutional, the invisible versus the visible concept of the church. But it will be readily seen that the application of these categories to the Book of Acts and to the opposing concepts of the church as seen in the Catholic, Protestant, and Baptist views cannot help us finally. The distinctions between the visible and the invisible are not Biblical, but arose at that point in history (terms coined by Augustine, elaborated by the Reformers) where the church was no longer the *ekklesia* of the believers but began to include "sinners" also. The visible church was hence not considered identical in scope with the invisible, which is really the fellowship of the saints of all ages, i.e., the people of God. The latter, however, was considered present in the visible church, and classically, in the hierarchy and the sacraments, and in this sense was visible. But both the essence and scope were regarded as invisible to the natural eye. Hence the remarkable Catholic view that only the ecclesiastical structure or institution is fully the church.

Nor does the mere contrast of the spiritual with the institutional help us. For while the New Testament church is certainly not institutional, she is nonetheless not "merely" spiritual. She is also "visible" in the sense that the believers are gathered together visibly, engage in observable activity, and live in visible discipleship, mutually submissive to one another.

We are thus thrown back to examine the New Testament view anew. Where and what is the Church? How is the Church constituted? The consensus which runs through practically all of the interpretations noted is that the Church is supernatural in origin and essence. Pentecost makes this very clear in fact, just as does the epistle to the Ephesians in explanation, that Christ through the Spirit is the head of the Church "from whom the whole body, joined and knit together by every joint with which it is supplied . . . makes bodily growth and upbuilds itself in love" (Ch. 4:16).

Our real difficulty thus lies in the visible expression of the Church, in her subjective aspects, in her social manifestation. Can we accept the Catholic claim that the visible organism represented in the apostolate (papacy) is essential and constitutive to the Church? Can we say with the major Protestant groups that the Church is visible in the proclamation of the Word, and a constant and recurrent creation of the Spirit, and thus as German scholars have emphasized in recent years, an ever-new *Ereignis* (event)? Can we solve the problem by eliminating the Church as a visible manifestation on earth from our thinking, recognizing her as purely supernatural and eternal, thus accepting the individual as God's unit of redemptive work and the "church" on earth as a simple pragmatic society to facilitate religious activity? Or is the Church rather the people of God constituted by the creative work of the Spirit and the response by the faith of discipleship on the part of men?

This fourth possibility was clearly articulated for the first time in the modern context by the sixteenth-century Anabaptist-Mennonites. Two illustrations will suffice. At the Anabaptist-Zwinglian state church debate at Zofingen in 1532, the spokesman of the latter asked the former, "Do you believe that there is one common unique holy Christian Church hidden in the whole world among all believers in which also the Holy Spirit performs his activation and exercise to the whole world as from the beginning?" To this the Anabaptist spokesman replied, "Yes, among the believers who submit themselves to the Spirit of God, among them God reigns and the Holy Spirit . . . ." Menno Simons very clearly held the same position. In his literary debate with Gellius Faber—the Catholic priest who became the Lutheran minister at Emden, Germany—Menno charged that despite his admission that the Church "has become drowsy, inattentive, ungrateful, and an apostate of Christ, has enraged God, and fallen into all manner of wickedness and sins," yet Faber "claims that she remains the church of Christ, *as if the church was inherited by one generation from another, and did not consist in faith, Spirit, and power* . . . . " (*Works II*, 91—italics added). "Therefore," Menno continues, "observe that which I write, and let it be to you a certain rule, namely, where the Spirit, word, sacraments, and life of Christ are found, that there the Nicene article comes in, 'I believe in the holy Christian church, the communion of saints, etc.' " (It should be noted that Menno's use of the term *sacrament* is "non-sacramental.")

Whether, as is sometimes argued, particularly by Dutch Anabaptist scholars, Menno in later life became more ecclesiastical need not concern us here. What Menno does assert is that the Church is to be found where men respond to the Holy Spirit. Thus both the objective Spirit and the subjective response of obedient faith are constitutive. This response, however, is neither mere inner experience nor individualism (cf. above, the Baptist view). Nor is the Church invisible. Common participation in the Spirit is the *koinonia* (fellowship) of the saints, and where they meet in *koinonia*, the Church is truly, fully, and visibly the Church. It should be noted that the above "rule" of Menno echoes the first description of the Church after Pentecost where disciples "devoted themselves to the apostles' teaching and fellowship, to the breaking of bread and prayers" (Acts 2:42).

We are therefore led to reject the three views regarding the Church in her manifestation on earth as noted earlier in this paper: (1) the Catholic, that the visible structure is the constitutive factor; (2) the "Protestant," that the message (Word and sacrament) is the constitutive factor; and (3) the typical "free church" view as illustrated in the Baptist statement, that the Church is purely a non-historical, spiritual reality, that the empirical "church," while beneficial, is nonessential, since the individual is the unit of God's relation to mankind (cf. above, p. 61). But by the same token we must reject the contemporary (American) Mennonite assumption that the overarching denominational organization, together with uniformly binding culture traits, is constitutive. This is especially true where conference structures have assumed an ecclesiastical "reality" which transcends the local assembly. It is to be seen in the unscriptural designation, "Mennonite Church." It is to be seen in the Mennonite inability to fellowship with Christians of other denominational affiliation, at least in the Lord's Supper. It is to be seen in the strong tendency to develop a denominational structure of clerics and even a hierarchy. Some of these tendencies are more than a century old; others are of more recent date.

To reject the above concepts of the Church is not to say that there are no Christians, and hence not *the Church*, within their scope. It is to say, however, that man-made strictures have been placed upon the work of the Spirit-created and believer-experienced *koinonia*. It is to recognize further that in all of these cases men have yielded to the subtle temptation to which the Church in history has always been subjected. Precisely because the Church *is* visible, men confuse the visible expression with the reality itself, in this way, that they believe that these expressions can be "inherited from one generation to another" by external means and that the Spirit must adjust Himself to these "cultural" structures. Now precisely this has been for centuries the Catholic dogma. Outside the visible church, namely, the whole social structure coming to a climax in the papacy, there is no salvation. And Protestantism finds it easy to revert into a mild form of this, since it never succeeded in breaking away from it. On the one hand, it rejected papacy, but on the other, unable or unwilling to accept the believers' church, it could not condition the Church on the response of obedient faith. The immediate solution was concentration on Word and sacrament. But those Protestants who in the conflict with the power structures of established (Protestant and Catholic) "churches" broke with the concept of all visible objectivity, ended as we have seen, without any real concept whatsoever of the Church in her subjective realization. The greatest tragedy of all, however, is to be found in those groups who had recaptured the New Testament concept and have become "catholic" in the course of time. Of such movements, the good Episcopalian clergyman, Samuel Shoemaker, has the following to say:

> I think we may say that the Church on its organized side must be allowed to be watchful and on guard—conservative in the right sense. But by the time an informal movement has grown 'conservative,' *its usefulness is probably over. The most backward-looking, out-of-date thing in the world is the radical movement become respectable* [italics added]. A formal Church most of us understand, but a formal informal group is as contradictory as it sounds. . . . The old organized Church, for all the stiffness of its joints, will have a more comprehensive view than such a dying movement." (*The Power of God*, Harper, 1954, p.145)

How the Church, the gathered believers, who live by the Spirit and in obedient faith, comes into realization and perpetuates herself is further treated in the following essays. It need only be added here that the catalogs of Church gifts or offices listed in the New Testament make the distinction which we have sought to point out very clear. In Acts 20:28 Paul tells the Ephesian elders that they have been made overseers *in* the flock and not *over* the flock as KJ mistakenly but naturally (for a state-church edition) translates. "In the church at Antioch there were prophets and teachers" (Acts 13:2). "And *God* has appointed *in* the church first apostles, second prophets. . . ." (I Cor. 12:28). But in the same context it is indicated that, "You are the body of Christ and individually members of it." The Christian is thus a member *of*, exercising a gift *in*, the Church. Peter admonishes the elders to recognize that they are not lords over the flock but examples to it. And finally, Christ Himself says, lordship is a thing of the Gentiles, not to be found among the disciples. That the pope has assumed the title "Servant of the Servants of God" is a fitting commentary on what has happened to his followers.

Biblicism and the Church

David A. Shank and John Howard Yoder

I. The Problem Defined

There is no doubt that the intention of Mennonites is to guide both thought and life by the Bible. Further, the conviction of Mennonites is generally that, in their present pattern of thought and life, they are doing so, at least as far as concerns their goals, although of course realizations may fall short. John A. Hostetler's *Mennonite Life* resumes this attitude by saying, ". . . behind all this surface diversity Mennonites possess a single idea. That idea is Bible-centeredness."

This central concern of Bible-centeredness must always be our starting point in thinking about the Christian faith and life. In the devotional life of the individual Christian, and within the bounds of a well-defined and broadly accepted Mennonite tradition, it is unnecessary to go into much detail to define just what that will mean. Yet it is becoming more and more clear that, in the interest of our concern for Biblicism, we must learn to state more clearly what we mean by that concept.

The non-Mennonite who reads the sentences quoted above will probably react by asking, "Then what about the Baptists? . . . or the Open Bible churches? . . . or the Pentecostals?" Such a reaction would be justified, for the hard fact is that Christendom is full of people and denominations claiming to believe the Bible and nothing but the Bible, yet disagreeing with each other. Even Mennonites cannot fully agree among themselves, as is shown when our quotation mentions "surface diversities." The shortcoming here cannot be the Bible's; it must be ours, and part of it lies in our not thinking through seriously enough what it means to be "Biblicists." Especially in our day, when other Christian groups are as never before open to certain elements of our Mennonite witness (as for example the nonresistant testimony), we must be especially clear as to what we mean by the claim to be Biblically grounded.

One aspect of this problem is the contrast between the Mennonite position and that of so-called Fundamentalist churches, which generally reject what has historically seemed to Mennonites to be clear Biblical teaching as to war or the oath, in the field of ethics, or as to feet-washing and the covering in the field of forms of worship, at the same time that they proclaim militantly their loyalty to the doctrine of Inspiration.

A second aspect lies in the trend of general theological thinking in the larger churches, both in systematic theology and in Biblical interpretation, away from liberalism toward a greater appreciation for the Bible's reliability and authority. This opens up a possibility of contact and witness toward circles with which for generations communication has been impossible because of liberalism and destructive criticism. Yet this movement "back to the Bible" does not come all the way back; a long list could be made of ways in which leading theologians accept the Bible as an authority, but not quite; with relation to them as well as to Fundamentalists we must be clear about the sense in which we accept the Bible.

The third aspect of the problem, and the most serious in many ways, is the missionary situation. New mission converts, unspoiled by accumulated traditions and prejudices, but also un-oriented, are ready to listen to God's teaching, and dismayed to find various missionaries who understand that teaching in contradictory ways. Whether it be in Brussels or London, where people ask, "Why another kind of evangelical mission?" or in Asia where the "young churches" begin to wonder why they are divided denominationally, the problem is the same; we must be clear as to our starting point for teaching and discussion. The arising of this problem is tied to the aggressiveness of a church in witness to other Christians and in missions; as already said, in the normal life of a non-evangelistic traditional church it would never become bothersome. The very fact that we raise it is thus a sign of life. The writer of these lines personally supports the Mennonite position as in the main Biblical; this does not however get rid of the need to explain and defend it more clearly for the convert or the non-Mennonite.

A fourth reason for special concern with this problem is the interest, shared by all Mennonites in diverse ways, in discipleship. Though the general use of this term in English is not old, the concept has always been central in the Anabaptist-Mennonite movement. The attitude which it designates may be summarily defined as follows:

- Obedience: God's purpose with man is not only pardon; He calls men to do His will. That will may be known and followed.

- Communion: The Christian's obedience is not a matter of servility but of life in the presence of God, who accomplishes by His indwelling Spirit what would otherwise be impossible.

- Imitation: The Christian's obedience is not a matter of applying codified rules whose foundation he ignores. The model for the life God wants is revealed in the Person of Christ, who calls us to follow Him.

- Cross: The Christian's obedience is most crucial at the point where good encounters evil. Discipleship, conformity to the example of Christ, requires him to accept suffering rather than to return evil for evil. The love revealed at the Cross is the final and most central authority for Christian behavior.

The ethical seriousness which discipleship involves has often manifested itself in a high degree of attentiveness to "minor" commands of Scripture. The term "all things" has in some circles become a label to designate this attitude. Further, if discipleship is not a purely personal matter, it will also involve some sort of discipline in the church. All of this renders doubly important an agreement about our understanding of Biblicism.

The easiest explanation would be to say that we obey all (Matt. 28:18–20) Biblical commands.[1] Already this answer is one possible definition of Biblicism, and one which lays us open to a serious charge of legalism. Yet it is not an adequate answer, for there are Biblical commandments which Mennonites as a whole do not apply literally, and there are other principles, not clearly commanded in Scripture, which

---

1. "The genius of Mennonitism has been to reject completely the traditional distinction between those New Testament commandments on the one hand which are binding both in form and spirit upon Christians for all time, and those on the other hand which are to be observed only in spirit . . . and to stress the parity of all New Testament commands" (J. C. Wenger, *Glimpses*, 149; cf. Paul Erb, "What It Means to Be a Mennonite," 24).

Mennonites as a whole do not apply literally, and there are other principles, not clearly commanded in Scripture, which have for many Mennonites the force of law. In the first category, the Scriptural commands which are not generally applied, we may list a few samples: Jesus' teaching against accumulating earthly wealth, against lending money for interest (or even expecting the principal back), His instructions not to carry money or a change of clothes; Peter's teaching against braided hair, Paul's requirement that a person ordained as bishop should have children of a certain age, his instructions to "drink a little wine." In the other category, commands without clear New Testament basis, we have strict positions on the use of instrumental music in worship, on clothing styles, on the exclusion from communion of members of other churches, on the inadmissibility of members' doing noncombatant military service, or abstinence from the use of beverage alcohol.

In citing these examples the intention is not to criticize the predominant Mennonite position on any one of these points; very good arguments may be brought for not applying literally some of the commandments cited, as well as for making an issue of some of those matters on which Scripture is silent. But the point we must admit is that, in bringing these arguments, we are practicing a kind of Biblical interpretation which we might not like to have others use on some of those other particular injunctions which Mennonites refer to as the "all things." The fact that "braided hair," discouraged by the New Testament, is now generally approved by Mennonites, springs from the obvious fact that the term has, in our culture, a meaning different from the one it bore in first-century Mediterranean civilization. Yet the devotional head covering, the practice of washing feet, and the meal of bread and wine also had specific meanings in that civilization which they do not have now, and still it is argued that Mennonite Biblicism requires maintaining as nearly as possible the original form. There are explanations for this difference; but these are not explanations which are self-evident, and the very need for explanations is proof enough that we must be more clear about what we mean by Biblicism.

Saying that "We believe in following all New Testament commandments" not only raises the serious question of legalism; it not only fails to explain the choices Mennonites make in following in different ways different kinds of commandments; it also fails to answer a more important question, namely, what our attitude should be to

New Testament *practice*, toward the *example* of the apostolic church. The direct instructions given in the New Testament epistles are often either generalities (like, "Wives, be subject to your husbands," or "Love one another"), or quite peripheral (like, "Drink a little wine"); yet we know much more, by inference from the epistles and directly from Acts, about the practice of the early church, under the leadership of the Spirit through the apostles and prophets. In such matters (form of worship, church order, and discipline, for example) are we to consider the New Testament example as meaningless for us because there is no specific command to follow it? Or as an example to be copied slavishly? To take either of these positions, or to try to find one between the two, would show what we mean by Biblicism. This is therefore the first question we must try to answer.

On one hand there is the position that times have changed, that we are no longer in the apostolic age, and that the way the apostolic church behaved is of no help to us. This seems to be, in so far as this writer can tell, the view of most (Old) Mennonite leaders and Bible teachers with respect to the early Church's form of church government, to the practice of frequent communion, to the practice of baptism soon after conversion, and to the rather disorganized form of meeting which prevailed in New Testament times. Those are questions, one would tell us in most Mennonite churches, concerning which we are not bound by the New Testament example. We may consider it instructive, but not normative.

Yet there is something unsatisfactory about such an answer. It seems both superficial and arbitrary to consider as not binding the New Testament usage on such a point as the frequency of the Lord's Supper, which was so obvious as to be taken for granted and never to need to be said in an epistle, and yet to take very seriously marginal questions on which an apostle gave specific detailed instructions because the answer was not obvious, and the Christians of Corinth or Thessalonica had to ask for guidance. Even if it seems inoffensive to those who are used to it, such a principle of interpretation is a hindrance to entering into contact with the mounting number of Christians and Biblical scholars who, without accepting in detail what seems to them a mechanical and legalistic literalism, nevertheless consider the New Testament example, as a whole pattern of life, as still exemplary for us.

From a historical point of view, it should be noted that it was in the realm of general practice (form of worship, form of church order, concepts of communion and baptism), and not in the realm of specific commands (devotional head covering, feet-washing, anointing), that the development away from the early church pattern took place, leading finally to Catholicism, where the specific commands are still honored. If we agree with Catholicism that the New Testament example is not binding where there is no express command, we have much less foundation to condemn the modifications which led to Catholicism. And if we consider some adaptations as legitimate (those made by Mennonites) and others not (such as those made by Catholicism), it is still more indispensable to know by what principles of interpretation such a distinction is justified.

A second point worthy of notice historically is that this distinction between New Testament commands, which are binding, and New Testament practice, which is not, was not the original Anabaptist-Mennonite view, as far as the present state of research indicates. Both were considered as authoritative by the Anabaptists. The Schleitheim Confession appeals both to apostolic teaching and to apostolic usage for support of its view on baptism (Art. 1). Menno Simons would accept either New Testament teaching or usage in support of Catholic doctrine and practice, if anyone could show him the proof.[2] There is at present a debate in scholarly circles about the idea of "restitution," i.e., in how far the Anabaptists thought they *were* the early church restored; but that is another question. That the New Testament pattern, in so far as they understood it, was taken as authoritative for their own faith and life, even on points where there was no specific Biblical command, has not been challenged. This attitude carries down to the present day in the practice, preserved by some Old Order Amish, of reading through the Book of Acts once a year, thus giving to the life of the beginning church a highly disproportionate amount of attention in comparison to other parts of the New Testament.

We must further recognize the obvious fact, so self-evident that we fail to take sufficient account of it, that if the New Testament example is

2. "If anyone under the canopy of heaven can show us from the Scriptures that Jesus Christ, the Son of the Almighty God, the eternal wisdom and truth, whom alone we acknowledge as the lawgiver and teacher of the New Testament, has commanded one word to that effect, or that His holy apostles have taught *or practiced* the like, then there is no need of an attempt to compel us by tyranny or torture. Only show us God's Word and our matter is settled. For we seek nothing else. . . . " (Menno Simons in *Mennonites in Europe*, 355–56).

not normative, some other tradition is. If we do not pattern our church life after the early church, we pattern it after some other church. That other church which then becomes the basic point of reference, be it the Mennonite church of a given time and place, or some other tradition, comes thus to have a greater normative authority than the apostolic church. This is difficult to justify Biblically, to say the least.

The argument that the New Testament practice must be adapted to suit our times and needs calls for two qualifications. One is the fact that the specific commands of the New Testament are just as dated as is the usage; if the need for adaptation applies to one it must by the same reasoning apply to the other as well.

But it is more important to ask whether, as a matter of historical fact, the changes which were made, leading to the adoption of forms and practices different from the New Testament example, really were made as conscious efforts to adapt to new situations in the most spiritual and faithful way. When the change was made, was it conscious and was it guided by principle? This is a question of history. If it can be demonstrated how the changes were introduced, in response to what cultural needs and changed situations, and in fidelity to what principles, then those deviations can at least be respected, whether or not we would judge them to have been right. Yet such a demonstration would be difficult to provide, either for the Catholicism which modified the New Testament attitudes to church order, form of worship, communion, and baptism, or for those aspects of Mennonite tradition which also modify, in other ways, the primitive pattern (communion only twice annually, baptism only after a long instruction period, fixed order of worship; on church order we shall say more later). And if a conscious, Spirit-led, Scripture-illuminated group decision was not behind the change, then the argument about the necessity of adaptation to fit new needs is not relevant and cannot justify a change made for other reasons. As to the changes which led to Roman Catholicism, we would tend to attribute more importance to pagan influences than to the leading of the Holy Spirit; whether the modifications leading to present Mennonite practices were made in the Spirit-led days of sixteenth-century Anabaptists or in the less aggressive Mennonitism between 1600 and 1850 is a serious question.

We have seen thus far:

- The need for a clearer idea of Biblicism in order to present to the world and to other Christians a clear witness for discipleship;
- The inadequacy of simply saying that we obey all New Testament commands, since they are not all applied in the same way, and some that are obeyed are not as clear in the New Testament as others;
- The inadequacy of an attitude to New Testament practice which draws a sharp line between that which is commanded expressly and what is not. It is the writers' conviction that a solution to this threefold need must be found if the Mennonite churches are to traverse the adjustments of the coming decades without losing the talent which the Lord has given them. To find this solution and to live it in our day will take renewed faithfulness to the Biblicism of the Anabaptists; it will take a renunciation of the pride with which Mennonites sometimes claim to be the only really Biblical Christians; and it will take the humility to be led by the Spirit, the Scripture, and the brethren, to keep our faithfulness both up-to-date and back-to-the-Bible. It is the purpose of these pages to encourage some careful thinking-in-fellowship toward that end, with the hope that others will provide confirmation and correction in the proper proportions.

II. Historical Background of the Discussion

Since the very existence of the Anabaptist-Mennonite movement is a result of a difference of opinion as to what Biblicism means, it will be useful to survey historically the development of the problem in order to understand the various positions as they were worked out, especially in Reformation times.

The starting point of church history is the New Testament church. Some aspects of the thought and life of this church, based on deep convictions about principle, were so self-evident that we do not find them explicitly taught in the New Testament (meeting on Sunday, not worshiping Caesar or idols), but simply presupposed. Other aspects we find treated in detail, because they were new to Jews (the Christian attitude to circumcision) or to Gentiles (sexual morality). Some were taken over from Judaism with little question or explicit teaching (baptism, the office of elder). Some questions are not treated for the simple reason that they never came up (use of musical instruments in worship, members entering military service). On some points we find recommendations (celibacy, not eating meat offered to idols when it bothers someone else), on others we find commands (basic questions of morality and discipline, nonresistance, work, love, unity, etc., as well as peripheral questions a church happened to ask about). All of these aspects of the church's life, in whatever degree of clarity or detail we find them reported or commanded, combined to form the life of the apostolic church. All of them, except perhaps some of the recommendations given in a qualified way (as celibacy), were considered by early Christians, under apostolic leadership, as the way they expressed their faithfulness to Christ, their discipleship.

The change which in the next five centuries led to what we know as Roman Catholicism applied to every facet of this original pattern: ethics, church order, form of worship, doctrine. The real reason, as we see it, for most of these changes, was a gradual loss of vigilance and vision which then permitted a progressive infiltration of pagan attitudes and practices. The other interpretation, however, is that times were changing, Christianity was gradually conquering the Roman world and carrying out its mission, so that with a changing situation adaptation was needed, which the Church, with Christ's authorization (Matt. 16), is empowered to carry out, the authority of the apostles being transmitted by them to the bishops and notably to the bishop of Rome.

Even Catholicism, however, set limits to its own authority, theoretically at least, by the establishment of the canon, i.e., the list of writings considered apostolic. The formation of the canon does not mean, as Catholic apologists argue, a claim of the church to be sovereign to Scripture, as if it would have been in its power to canonize any other list of writings instead; it means rather that the Roman Church, during and in spite of its growing independence from Scripture, recognized the uniqueness of the apostolic writings and assented to their apostolicity, thus setting a limit to Rome's own ability to "bind and loose."[3] Even though Catholicism later did not respect this limit, its having been pronounced still preserved a form of Biblicism which was the opening wedge of the Reformation.

3. This distinction is especially brought out by O. Cullmann in his *Tradition*.

Luther, the first Reformer and the one who stayed closest to Catholicism (except for the Anglican Church, which does not concern us here), understood Biblicism as meaning the elimination of anything, in the traditional Catholic pattern, which was clearly condemned in the Bible. Those elements not condemned could be kept. Luther's eyes were closed to much of the Bible's teaching by two other assumptions, which he never really examined consciously to see whether they were condemned or commanded. One was the concept of the unity of church and society, which brings with it infant baptism, the state church, war, the oath, and a minimum level of morality. The other assumption was that the Bible's main concern was the doctrine of justification by faith; this kept him from discovering that the Bible is really most interested in discipleship. These factors combined to make of Lutheranism a kind of minimum Biblicism, seeking not so much the fullest obedience as the avoidance of disobedience. As a result, orthodox Lutheranism has changed little from the sixteenth century to the present. Pietism likewise, and neo-orthodoxy in another way, by limiting the Gospel to forgiveness, weaken the authority of the Bible for discipleship.

The Reformed tradition, which took shape gradually from the time of Zwingli and Oecolampad to that of Calvin, went farther than Luther in the return to Biblicism. Instead of simply dropping from Catholic tradition those things which the Bible forbids, the Reformed sought to eliminate everything which was not supported by Scripture (this statement is an oversimplification but not an unfair one). One example was the elimination of music from worship, with the exception of the Psalms; another was a more critical attitude toward statues, and toward the hierarchical church order. The reason for this difference is not fully clear, but might lie partly in the greater degree of humanistic education among the Reformed leaders, in contrast to the more scholastic and monastic background of the Lutherans.

At any rate this more positive view of Biblicism enabled the Reformed churches, with the passing of time, to grow continually closer to the Biblical ideal. Like the Lutherans', their understanding was at first hindered by their unquestioned acceptance of the unity of church and society, with the same immediate results (infant baptism, war, oath) as for the Lutherans; yet their insistence on Scriptural authority and the need for constant reformation left them open to later improvement. Already from the time of Zwingli to that of Calvin there is change, for instance, in the attitude of submission of church to state; in Calvin's system the church, although not yet separated from the state, is at least far less dependent. The Reformed churches were also open, in the nineteenth century, to revival movements which led to a renewed appreciation of the priesthood of all believers and to a new warmth of personal piety, as well as, in some places in France and Switzerland, to separation from the state. And now in our time it is in the Reformed tradition that a new Biblical renewal is going on, with serious criticism of infant baptism and a re-evaluation of the meaning of the ministry, as well as a new respect for nonresistance. In all of these respects, we can only welcome this development toward a position which is more Biblical, and we must therefore respect the kind of Biblicism which can lead in that direction, all the while regretting that it took so long.

The Anabaptists were an outgrowth not of Catholicism nor of Lutheranism, but of the Reformed movement. Just as we have seen that the Reformed leaders were more thorough in their criticism of Catholicism than the Lutherans, so the first Anabaptists were more thorough than Zwingli. This came to the surface at two points. First was the identity, which was unchallenged by the Reformers, of church and society. The Anabaptists, through their experiences in Zurich from 1523 to 1525, learned to reject this assumption, and that rejection made it possible for them to apply consistently Scriptural teaching on baptism, nonresistance, the oath, and discipleship in general.

The other issue was the relationship of the two Testaments. The Reformed movement took all of the Bible on the same level, as does modern Fundamentalism. This meant that the ultimate authority lay in the book, rather than in the uniqueness of the Incarnation and the apostolic witness of the New Testament. The Anabaptists on the other hand maintained the absolute supremacy of Christ and the apostles as authority, not only over against the later church, but also over against the earlier revelation in Judaism. The honest reading of the New Testament confirms its claims to supremacy over the Old, as does evangelical theology, but the Anabaptists were the only Biblicists of their time to be consistent in applying this insight. The only Reformation Christians to apply the Bible's own criticism to these two questions of the church-society relationship and the inter-testamental relationship, the Anabaptists were thus the only reformers truly faithful to the Reformed intention.

III. Principles of Consistent Biblicism

We have seen that the first original contribution of the Anabaptists to the redefinition of Biblicism was the fact that, both more spiritual and more thoroughly logical than the Reformers, and also less committed to the maintenance of the existing institutional order, they perceived the unquestioned assumptions which were guiding the Reformers' thinking, and rejected, most basically, those attitudes growing out of the identification of church and society. This question no longer needs to be faced in the same form, but the basic problem remains in other manifestations, with other similar assumptions needing to be unmasked and rejected as un-Biblical, among others the belief, shared by all sorts of Americans from *Sunshine Magazine* through Dulles and Luce to the K.K.K., that Protestantism and American patriotism belong together. The ease with which Spellman and McCarthy put Catholicism in the same framework makes it all the more evident that we must begin by defining the true goals and assumptions of those with whom we discuss. This preliminary analysis of partly unconscious presuppositions is the first step toward a consistent Biblicism.

The second principle is the insistence on the unique authority of the Incarnation as attested by the apostolic writings, i.e., the New Testament. Neither the partial revelation of the Old Testament nor the decisions of church authorities since New Testament times (even the Nicene confession) can be permitted to interfere with that authority. The authority for faith is the Person of Christ, to whom the apostolic writings give reliable testimony.

Thirdly, we must not hesitate to utilize the fruits of the last century's historical, archaeological, and linguistic study of the New Testament texts. Much such study was discredited because, in reaction to the obscurantism of orthodoxy, whose scholastic doctrine of Inspiration would not permit the texts to speak for themselves, some Biblical scholars made highly preposterous claims under the name of "Biblical criticism." These claims have now collapsed, not because Fundamentalists reacted emotionally to them, but because they were not based on the texts, so that honest objective study showed them to be ungrounded, and demonstrated again the reliability of the apostolic witness. On almost everything that really matters, New Testament exegetes have come to a great degree of agreement as to what the New Testament means by what it says, and what the life of the New Testament church was like. It is not at all exaggerated to claim that, thanks to the tools now available for Biblical study, we can now understand the intent of the New Testament better than the Christians of A.D. 200 or any time since then. Even unbelieving scholars must today admit, on the basis of objective study of the texts, the New Testament's claim to authority, and the nature of its teaching. This is not to say that Christians in the time between A.D. 200 and the recent past could not understand the Bible enough for all their needs of piety, doctrine, and discipleship, nor to deny that the Spirit of God can and did reveal Himself to all those who sought Him; yet the fact remains that one of the strongest witnesses for discipleship in modern Christendom (and thus the clearest understanding of the New Testament's real concern) comes, not from the traditional advocates of an orthodox doctrine of Inspiration, but from the exegetical theologians who have the scholarly equipment to read the Bible with both microscope and telescope; men like Cullmann and Eichrodt in Europe, Taylor, Rowley, Hunter, and Stewart in England, Minear, Miller, and Bright in the States.

Fourthly, we must question seriously the validity of a distinction of level between New Testament command and example. We have the commands we have because the Christians at Corinth happened to ask Paul for advice about certain problems and Paul's answer was preserved; there is no reason to think that the things the Corinthians did not ask about, or about which the apostle's answer was not preserved, had apostolic sanction in any lesser degree. Both command and example were time-bound in that they represented responses to problems in first-century surroundings; both command and example were based on principle. If the commands are considered inflexible there seems to be no logical argument (except the most slavish legalism) for considering example as subject to change; if practice can be modified to fit new situations, so logically may the form in which we apply given commands (cf. the example of "braided hair" already cited).

Fifthly, we must be clear as to what sort of modifications of New Testament example might be legitimate on the grounds of need to adjust to a changing world. For a change to be valid, we should require at least the following essentials:

- The change must be made by a studied and prayerful decision of the brotherhood. Changes into which a church slips almost unconsciously or without the leaders' having properly consulted the brotherhood cannot be Biblically justified, however convincing the arguments might be to individuals.

- There must be clarity as to the principle involved in the New Testament ideal, whether command or practice, and clarity as to why that principle is no longer served by the form of expression which, in New Testament times, was adequate. Then there must be clarity as to the new proposal's being a faithful expression for our time of the same principle. It is not sufficient to consider a New Testament form as out of date; there must be the conviction that the principle is not sacrificed by the change, but rather served more faithfully. To use again the relatively innocent example of "braided hair, " we may be certain that the condemnation of braids in the New Testament was an expression of simplicity and of nonconformity to worldly fashions and sensuality; we may be just as certain that in our day some of the simplest and most non-conformed hairdresses are those based on the braid; thus we may confidently affirm that by changing completely the formal, literal expression of a clear Biblical command, we are being as faithful as possible to the principle expressed in the original injunction. An example in the other direction would be the use of bread and wine in communion, which has much less meaning apart from first-century dietary and worship practices. Yet we have found no better substitute; so we take the trouble, rightly, of learning all we can in order to understand the full meaning of that out-of-date practice.

- The question must not be "Is it forbidden?" when a new proposal arises. That would be a reversion to a Lutheran concept of Biblicism and a sacrifice of discipleship to legalism. The question is never "Is it permitted?" but "Does it edify?" (I Cor. 10:23). We should not ask whether a change in church order, in form of worship, or in ethics is forbidden; we should ask what is the spiritual principle whose faithful application requires that innovation. This same attitude applies to the extension of New Testament principles to problems not directly dealt with in the New Testament; those extensions, examples of which we mentioned earlier (conscientious objection, temperance, abstinence), are to be evaluated by asking the same questions: Is the application conscious? Is it made by the brotherhood? Is it positively based on New Testament principle?

Sixthly, the presence of a pattern of faith and life which is perfectly conformed to New Testament command and example is not a sign of the true church, nor is deviation from the apostolic model a sure sign of the absence of the true church. (This is the Roman Catholic answer!) Especially do we need both charity and humility toward those who, having gone through other developments than we, both in spiritual growth and in reasoning, have not accompanied us in the process of decision and application in which we feel to have been divinely led. The expression of this humility will be the willingness to go back repeatedly and examine both logically and historically that process of leading, always asking, "Was it conscious (of everything involved)? Was it done by the (whole) brotherhood? Was it positively based on New Testament principle?"

Legalism, in the sense in which the New Testament condemns it, involves the assumption that we can judge and act, either positively in the sense of declaring it meritorious, or negatively in the sense of declaring it sinful, on the basis of a rule about the act itself, without asking whether the person acting knew about the rule, agreed with it, understood it, or not. We may be ever so convinced about the moral rightness or wrongness of the act itself (e.g., military service), and we should be; but that gives us no authority to suspend charity or fraternity toward people who commit that act without knowing about or understanding how we reached that conviction, or who respond to the problem in a situation basically different from ours. We shall deal with this problem in detail later

IV. The Ministry in the New Testament

To illustrate what is meant by Biblicism as here defined, the effort will be made here to summarize briefly what we learn from the New Testament as to the ministry in the early church, both in command and example. Then current problems of application in Mennonite circles will be approached from the perspective of the claim that this command and example remains a valid point of reference.

The foremost kind of minister mentioned in the New Testament is beyond doubt the apostle. The apostle's ministry is based on the call and choice of Christ (Acts 1:2), and his authority is that of a witness of Christ's work and resurrection (Acts 1:21, 22; Luke 1:2; I John 1:1–3). The ministry of the apostle is unique and can never be duplicated in other men. Menno Simons' favorite verse (I Cor. 3:11), in comparing Paul's work with that of other ministers, says in effect, "Anyone can build on the foundation, and will be judged by the quality of his work; but the work which *I* did *as apostle* among you, the laying of the foundation, the testimony to the work and resurrection of Christ, can not be done otherwise than I did it, nor redone, for there is no other foundation." This means that although the apostolic authority in teaching, in ethical instruction, in church founding is final for all time, not everything about the (sometimes authoritative) way the apostles themselves acted in teaching, church management, or discipline, is necessarily exemplary for people who are not apostles. The authority which the apostles had in the church itself, which is the repository of the apostolic witness to Christ.

Secondly, we may speak of the "spiritual gifts." As the term indicates, these capacities (prophecy, tongues, healing, administration, liberality) are given by the Spirit, not conferred by the church. The church may recognize these gifts and channel their use (as for instance in asking prophets to await their turns and speakers in tongues to arrange for translation), but the church does not choose the holders of gifts, and in general we know nothing of formal ordination preceding their use. No specific gifts are commanded, since they are not a fruit of the human will, but their appearance is expected as a normal fruit of the Spirit's presence. There was no order of value attached to the various gifts, as is shown by the fact that the various lists found in the New Testament do not have the same contents nor the same order (Rom. 12; I Cor. 12; Eph. 4).

Thirdly, we may speak of certain "offices" or "ministries"; not in the sense of judicial status or professional prestige attached to a certain title or set of credentials, but simply in the sense of "gifts" which appear to have been crystallized into a functional concept, i.e., terms consistently used by the New Testament to designate a certain set of services. All of these offices are determined by the calling of the Holy Spirit and all appear to be confirmed by the church.

(a) We have the term *diakonos*, which is translated "servant" in the Gospels, "deacon" in the pastoral epistles, and "minister" in the other epistles. The title in the sense of a specific office is not used in Acts, and only tradition applies it to the seven who were ordained in Acts 6. Likewise only tradition supports the assumption that the task of the "deacons" was material aid, though there is no especial reason to assume that tradition is wrong. There is no indication of their receiving financial support, unless the widows whose "enrollment" is discussed in I Tim. 5 were deaconesses at the same time that they were recipients of charity.

(b) *Didaskalos*, "teacher," is an office which can overlap with that of apostle (I Tim. 2:7) or of elder (5:17). That it is thus separately mentioned demonstrates that it is a separate function not filled by all elders or apostles. Not all teachers are good (II Tim. 4:3), and there should not be too many of them (Jas. 3:1); the task is evidently that of teaching, instruction in the doctrinal elements of faith on the basis of the Old Testament and the apostolic witness. The teacher may justifiably receive material support, as his function is a full-time employment (or can be) involving technical skills (I Tim. 5:17, 18; Gal. 6:6).

(c) The "evangelist was presumably comparable to the modern bearer of that name. His work is to evangelize, i.e., to carry the Gospel message to non-Christians. As this ministry may involve traveling, it is right of him to expect support from those who send him or those who accept his message (Matt. 10:10; Luke 10:7; Rom. 16:1, 2; I Cor. 9:1-18; Titus 3:13). In some ways the place of the evangelist is most like that of the apostle (though all of the offices here named were combined in the apostolic charge), in that he has the initial responsibility of teaching and instituting church order where there was no church before. As soon, however, as a church is set up, there is no reason for his quasi-apostolic authority over it to continue, and he will either turn to other pagans, remaining an evangelist, or take the status of teacher within the new congregation.

(d) We also encounter the term "prophet"; to prophesy is to speak a word to the present need of the church (I Cor. 14:1-5). It does not however seem to have been crystallized into a specific office like the terms mentioned earlier; it is a function recommended to everyone (*loc. cit.*), including women (11:5), but should be kept under control (Rom. 12:6; I These. 5:1; I Cor. 14:32). In post-apostolic writings we hear of the prophet as an itinerant preacher.

(e) Finally, we must consider a set of three terms. "Elder" (*presbyteros*), a term carried over from the Jewish synagogue, refers especially to *qualifications* of age, experience, and reputation. The second, "bishop" (*episcopus*), coming from Greek usage (meaning "overseer"), refers especially to the *function* of administration and leadership. The third, "shepherd" (pastor), associated with other terms like "sheep," "flock," refers figuratively to responsibility for spiritual nutrition and growth, what we commonly think of as pastoral care, edification, counseling. It is with reference to these terms and the office to which all three refer that there is the greatest difference between the New Testament pattern and the practices of the several branches of modern Christendom. For this office, for which we shall hereafter use the term "elder" for reasons of convenience, is the major office of the New Testament church after the apostles; and all three of the terms, bishop, pastor, elder, refer to the same charge. Acts 20 uses all three with reference to the same group of men, the leaders of the church at Ephesus. The three sets of ideas are also associated in I Peter 5 and Titus 1. Like the evangelist and teacher, the elder also takes over a part of the apostle's functions. New Testament use of the term is generally in the plural, leading to the very strong probability that there were as a rule several in each established congregation. The council of elders was charged with the pastoral oversight of the congregation, i.e., the spiritual leadership, ethical counseling, and the direction of worship. Elders were generally not supported, with the exception of those who served also as teachers (*loc. cit.*). Twice they are urged to serve without recompense (Acts 20:32–35; I Peter 5:2); these urgings indicate that there was a possibility that they might be supported partially.

The most striking conclusion to be drawn from this enumeration is the absence of two offices which are most characteristic in modern Christianity; the "pastor" in the sense of one professional minister leading a congregation, and the "bishop" in the sense of a minister with authority over several congregations. Both these terms were originally interchangeable with that of "elder," referring to one of several men who shared the leadership in a local council. Henri d'Espines, professor in Calvin's own Geneva University, drew the same conclusion, and has dared to say that Calvin's view of the pastoral office is un-Biblical, that "this state of affairs is deplorable," and that "the restoration of the collective pastorate, exercised by a veritable council of elders, is one of the primary conditions of the spiritual renewal which our churches need." Once again, we see Reformed Biblicism at its best coming out in favor of the authority of Scripture over the church, in a way to challenge the Biblicism even of Mennonites, on a point where the New Testament example is clear, in spite of the scarcity of direct commands.

V. The Ministry in the Contemporary Church

The concept of the ministry is one of the points where we see most clearly how artificial would be the distinction between New Testament example and command. There is a command to establish elders in every congregation; but there is no commanded definition of an elder; only in New Testament usage can we determine what the term means. To consider New Testament practice as not binding makes the command meaningless. It is thus only on the basis of the Anabaptist assumption that the early church's practice is normative for us that there can be any concern about the present question: how to apply our Biblicism to the concept of the ministry.

We turn first to the question of number; the New Testament church had several elders (bishops, pastors) in the average congregation. It might be added that such has also been the historical pattern in Switzerland, Alsace, and Lorraine, areas from which most American (Old) Mennonites come, although our present question is not one of Mennonite history. We must observe that such a pattern is no longer the rule in American Mennonitism. Many congregations have one sole minister; some have a group of trustees or a council, but such groups deal chiefly with business matters and think of themselves as laymen in contrast to the pastor, whose job they do not mean to share; others have a council of ministers and deacons but under a single bishop. Thus both the "pastor" and the "bishop" concept, in their non-Biblical modern meanings, have gained considerable ground at the expense of the New Testament "council" pattern.

On the basis of our criteria of consistent Biblicism, we must ask whether this development was conscious, was thought through by the whole brotherhood, and was decided on out of fidelity to New Testament principle. The argument that different times require adaptations is, as we have seen, logically useless unless it can be shown that a conscious adaptation, guided by principle, actually took place. Whether these conditions were met in the process which led to the present situation is open to serious question. Historically, much of this change seems to have come about with the division of large congregations into smaller units for convenience of meeting, but without giving the new congregations full congregational status or a complete ministry. This development in the nineteenth century was then followed in the twentieth by a movement in imitation of other churches using the "pastoral" pattern.

If the conditions for a valid adaptation were not met, what really happened was the unconscious and unjustifiable substitution of non-apostolic tradition for apostolic tradition. Even if one does not believe that apostolic tradition should be final authority, it would be hard to claim that non-apostolic tradition, uncritically adopted, is inherently better. The conclusion would seem therefore to be that, out of consistent Biblicism, Mennonites should seek to return in the most expeditious way to the New Testament pattern according to which the pastoral ministry—leadership, discipline, baptism, communion, visiting, ethical counsel and decision, exhortation, worship—is assured in each congregation by a council of elders, chiefly self-supporting, meeting the requirements of I Tim. 3.

Secondly, we turn to the question of ministerial support. We have seen that support is legitimate for the apostle, the teacher, and the evangelist, though even in those cases the conscientious solution might be not to take advantage of the right to support, as Paul often preferred. The task of elder, however, if not supplemented with that of teaching, does not generally call for support.

The need to support evangelists and missionaries is unquestioned in all our churches, though that support is not always adequate (judging by what the members consider "adequate" to keep for themselves). The teacher's function may well be thought of as including Bible study, catechism, Sunday-school teacher training, and doctrinal preaching (but most preaching should be prophetic, not doctrinal—I Cor. 14:5). If the minister's function is thought of in this way, to the exclusion of strictly pastoral charges, then full- or part-time support is both legitimate and desirable. But it should be kept in mind that such a specialized teacher is not what most congregations and most ministers have in mind when they approach the question of the supported ministry; they more often think of the "pastoral" concept as generally understood in Protestantism, which is a transfer of the prerogatives of the elders' council. At a time when Protestantism is learning, both from history and from the Bible, the inadequacy of that pastoral concept, it is regrettable to observe that not always do Mennonites keep clear the distinction between supporting professional teachers, which is Biblical, and paying professional pastors, which is not.

Mennonite tradition calls for the office of "preacher," subordinate to that of "bishop." It is significant that the oldest terms for this office, *Leerar* in Dutch and *Diener am Wort* in German, are terms which underline the teaching function of the office. Thus the traditional division between the function of preacher and bishop, though later often misconceived, sprang from a Biblical awareness of the importance of the teaching task as well as of the difference between that task and the pastoral responsibility.

Thirdly, we must evaluate the tendency, gaining ground rapidly in many quarters, toward calling seminary graduates as ministers. Is it Biblical? With respect to the matter of support, and the plurality of elders-pastors, we need only to refer to what has already been said. In other respects we must look further. The seminary graduate is usually young, which does not qualify him for the role of elder (I Tim. 3, significance of age, experience, reputation). He is trained in doctrine, which is a good thing, but such training is not a qualification for the office of pastor (elder); it should thus never be considered a prerequisite. And lastly, he is from outside the congregation to which he is called, in most cases. This would not disqualify him as an evangelist, and not necessarily as a teacher, but once again it keeps him from being what the New Testament thinks of as an elder.

We must ask whether the tendency toward a trained, supported young ministry has been undertaken consciously, by the whole brotherhood, in faithfulness to New Testament principle. The answer cannot be an unmixed *yes*, for the thinking has not been sufficient in either breadth or depth; but neither is the answer a clear *no*, for there exists the consciousness that this can bring about a momentous change, coupled with a sort of helplessness which sees no other way out. There is still reason to hope that with careful thought, to which these pages hope to contribute, this change can be understood in the light of the Bible, and the churches come to clarity on the conditions under which it is justifiable.

Without further dissecting matters of detail, let us have the nerve to take the New Testament at face value and tie together the loose ends of the discussion in a summary of guiding principles which we have no reason to consider as not valid for our time:

(a) The development toward the supported trained ministry is valid if the minister's function is clearly teaching, evangelism, or both, and if he has the gifts and calling therefore from the Holy Spirit.

(b) It is not valid if he either expects or is expected to take over pastoral functions. In his teaching function he should rather seek to lead the congregation to understand and to conform to the Biblical view of the pastorate as in the hands of a council of elders.

(c) We will ask both the seminaries and the young ministers to keep this distinction clear, and to aim at providing the churches with the specialized services which require, or are at least benefited by, advanced training.

(d) We will be careful about terminology—"Reverend, "clergy," "layman"—which betrays an unjustified conception of the pastorate, or a sacramental conception of ordination as making a man different from what he was before or from other men. Ordination is nothing but the congregation's obedient recognition of God's call and the authorization to exercise the gifts which the Holy Spirit has already granted.

(e) We will avoid excessive mobility and interchangeability in the ministry. We will prefer to call ministers—elders at any rate, teachers and evangelists if possible—from the midst of the congregation for a lifetime of service. The suggestion that call and ordination should precede training deserves serious consideration, though it could not be made a hard and fast rule.

(f) We may finally propose one clear and conscious adaptation to modern needs. The speed, complications, and paperwork of modern life (as well as congregation size, which is a question for debate in its own right) make it justifiable for the church to have a supported *secretary*; to record the deliberations of the council of elders, to deal with matters of correspondence and calendar. This might also be a part of the task of the supported minister, and not the least important.

Pragmatic arguments of psychology, ease of administration, and modernity may be adduced in favor of the New Testament ideal, or against it. Such arguments should be stated and evaluated, but for Biblicism they cannot be final. For this reason we omit for the moment the exposition of the numerous pragmatic and psychological grounds which seem to weigh in favor of a return to the Biblical pattern.

VI. The Institutional Problem

One of the areas in which it is easiest to find the New Testament inadequate is that which we now approach. We may define the outline of the problem best by illustration. It includes:

- the question of communion in relation to church organization: problems of intercommunion, close communion, and discipline.
- the question of organizational relations between congregations: the denomination, interchurch collaboration, and "ecumenical" activity.
- the question of polity: what is the real source of authority in the church?
- the question of "indigenosity": the relation between a daughter church's right to independence and its need for continuity, help, and control.
- the question of truth: Scriptural and creedal authority in interchurch doctrinal discussion.

For this whole problem, many would argue, it is futile to seek an answer in the New Testament, since the apostolic church had no such problems to deal with. The present paper attempts only to demonstrate that such is not the case. The New Testament church, from its very beginning, faced, and solved, the institutional problem in a way which is exemplary, and that example retains its validity for us unless there is proof to the contrary. This study will not attempt to deduce all the answers for our day from that example, but only to make plain that they can be found, by the use of one case history.

The case at hand is the question of the relations of Judaists and Hellenists in the early church, as we see them described in the second section of Acts and the first half of Galatians. The exegetical study itself, being lengthy, cannot be included here; if it were extended to the rest of the New Testament it seems sensible to suppose that even greater clarity would result, but already in a summary of what such a study teaches us we may find enough information to support our contention as to the relevance of the New Testament for institutional problems.

The sketchy study of these two sources with the sample they give us of the life of the primitive church makes it clear that there existed in that church two separate organizational setups and behind them four distinguishable tendencies (without going into the problem of schismatic elements in the Pauline churches, such as the four parties in Corinth).

The "main line" organizationally remains the Jerusalem church through the whole period. From Acts 6 onward its position in the story is passive, though obedient. It is willing to recognize the Spirit's initiative when Philip, then Peter, and then Paul are used to break down new barriers. This organization, which through the Twelve and Jesus' family maintained a historical continuity with the earthly Christ, however did not itself take the initiative toward expansion, and remained favorable toward the Temple worship.

The "main line" as far as the author of Acts is concerned is the one led by the Spirit, through a series of organizational irregularities; the Spirit continually forced innovations on the church, which the organization itself was not ready to undertake. Soon after Pentecost the Hellenists became the leaders of this movement; they are the first to break with established Judaism, the first to be persecuted, the first to do mission work outside of Jerusalem, the first to be called Christians, the first to understand the implications of Christology for the outreach to the Gentiles . This position was taken over by Paul at Antioch, and became New Testament Christianity as we know it.

Somewhere between these two lines is Peter. As missionary he is head of an evangelistic activity separate from that of Paul's, with whom however he agrees basically in doctrine. He remains subordinate to the Jerusalem church, which puts him in a strategically more delicate situation than Paul,

Fourthly, as a strong faction within the church at Jerusalem, there is the "party of the Pharisees" (Acts 15:5), whose belief is that Jesus was the Messiah expected by the faithful Jews. Their understanding of law is that of the Pharisees; so is their superficial view of the resurrection as little more than a proof of Messianity. Their worship continued to center in the Temple, and they could admit no abrogation of the ceremonial law. It was probably due to their reaction that James, the Lord's brother, the personification of continuity in the Messianic line, replaced Peter the missionary as head of the Jerusalem church. The Judaizers (another name for the same group) were willing to split a local church, or the whole church, in the interest of their concepts of continuity and faithfulness. They themselves were not persecuted, as were the Hellenists, by the Jerusalem authorities, for that persecution was not directed against the Christians as such but against those who undermined the ceremonial law. Their only interest in mission work was to make sure that the law was observed, and toward this end they sent delegates to visit Antioch and the Pauline churches.

The "Jerusalem agreement" was an attempt to reach an understanding between these two groups, which, however, turned out to he inadequate. The Judaists understood that agreement to authorize the division of the church definitively into a Hellenistic and a Judaistic branch. Paul understood it as simply the Jerusalem church's ratification of his ministry, so that he could continue to evangelize and remain in fraternal relations. The organizational arrangement was inadequate precisely because the real difference between the Hellenists (Paul) and the Judaists was Christological, having to do with the place of law in salvation.

Paul nevertheless accepted and worked with the institutional situation as given, with two separate organizations and an inadequate understanding between them. He accepted it as a fact, out of charity, and not as a principle. He lived up to his end of the agreement scrupulously, as is indicated by the collections he took for the Jerusalem church; but he never let the agreement and the division of fields be a barrier to fellowship on a local level or to his ministry. He continued to consider the Jerusalem church as his brethren and to administer corrections if needed. He writes the Roman church, which did not belong to his organization, though taking pains to introduce himself more fully than usual, and to apologize for his projected visit as well as for his clear instructions (Rom. 15:15–24). He maintains a clear distinction between the level of congregational discipline, on which he makes it clear that the Judaizers are to be treated as false teachers, and the level of intercongregational and mission organization, on which he goes out of his way to be brotherly, being in fact taken prisoner because of his second-mile respect for the ceremonial law.

From the position of Paul and the Hellenists, which triumphed both in history and in the canon, we may draw several conclusions as to ways of approaching the institutional problem in our time. These conclusions are presented as examples, with no attempt to be exhaustive. First and most superficially, we remark that the Roman church, claiming to base its authority on the primacy of Peter, has no Scriptural foundation. Peter was the chief of the Twelve at the beginning, and head of the Jerusalem church for only a short time. Later he headed the mission work of the Jerusalem church, but was subordinate to James and scolded by Paul.

More important, we have the demonstration that institutional continuity is not the essential definition of the church. The growth of the church had to break through the fetters of institutional continuity repeatedly. As more valid signs of the true church we may note the leading of the Spirit, the interest in evangelization, and the Christology of justification by grace. Other signs could also be found in other areas of the New Testament; but institutional continuity is not one of them.

No institutional line is valid as a guide for restricting fellowship to one part of the church. The idea "we have our church with our rules, you are free to have your church with your rules "was the one followed by the Judaists in their effort to split the Antioch congregation. The unity of the church, in the form of the united worship and communion of the Christians in a given locality, is not simply a psychological or aesthetic or organizational preference; it is a theological necessity. No organization (and already there were more than one) may interfere with the unity of the local or the total fellowship; Paul even insisted on giving expression to his unity with the Jerusalem church when he suspected that his expression of unity was not really wanted.

This is especially relevant to problems of intercommunion or close communion. Such problems can never be solved Biblically unless they are removed from the level of the denomination to be treated on the level of the congregation. There is considerable Biblical evidence for the exclusion from communion of certain categories of people—unbelievers and unrepentant fallen church members—but no justification for basing that exclusion on denominational adherence. We should further distinguish between those problems of communion which revolve around the validity of the sacrament (in a Catholic or Lutheran context) and those which concern the individual's right of access. In one case the denominational barrier to communion is a questionable concept of sacrament; in the other it is a concept of discipline; in both, the relationship between denomination and church is questionable.

In spite of the very limited validity of an organization's claims to authority, we owe existing organizations respect so long as, like the church under James, they permit the real work of the church to go on. Both the desire to have only one organization (the classic liberal conception of ecumenical relations) and the desire to have none, which means in the end having one more (so-called nondenominational churches), over esteem the organizational problem. Paul's answer was to let the organizational problem be solved on a purely functional basis by those who had time for such concerns, to respect that framework to the point of supporting it financially, but never to let it get in the way of his commission to preach his Gospel, nor of the essential unity of either a local congregation or the total Christian fellowship.

The extent of Paul's efforts to maintain relations with Jerusalem should teach us that we are not authorized to break off relations of fellowship, on a level other than that of congregational discipline, except when the initiative is not ours. The idea that breaking away from another church is a way to be faithful is sectarian in the strict sense of that word. The Zurich Anabaptists did not break away from the Zwinglian church in order to be faithful; they called the whole church to a commitment to discipleship, and only when the official church's refusal to obey was given the force of law did they feel obliged to set up a separate organization. As long as persecution continued, the Anabaptists were justified in calling the state church names. But now that, four centuries later, the Reformed churches of Switzerland are apologizing for the behavior of Zwingli and Calvin, there is no justification for continued refusal of fellowship, especially when that apology coincides with a readiness to accept the Bible's authority. Such a recognition would not involve organizational unity (since for practical reasons that would make no sense), nor would it mean any concessions on questions of truth; it would simply mean the re-establishment of a possibility of communication and occasional joint service or witness, which is the only real meaning of interchurch relations above the level of the congregation.

VII. The Denominational Problem

Our discussion of the institutional problem in general has already mentioned the denomination; we now turn more directly to the question of the rightful place of denominational organization. The existence of distinct "denominations" (Latin for "namings") with varying standards and teachings, with independent organizations and without mutual fellowship is externally a change from New Testament times, but as we have seen already it existed in germ in the Early Church, not only in the Judaistic controversy but also in Corinth (I Cor. 1:12). They were clearly condemned by the apostle when they interfered with fellowship, though they had not yet taken on forms as separate and mutually exclusive as exist in our day. We must first of all accept the Bible's condemnation of such a situation; but that acceptance does not provide a solution to the problem or even a way to live with it. We must therefore inquire further into the seat of authority in the New Testament church, or else attempt a purely pragmatic solution.

One current pragmatic solution takes the following line: Since we cannot be in fellowship with all churches, we shall accept the necessity of limiting our fellowship to those churches with which we are in substantial agreement . With them we will organize together our mission, education, publishing, and service work, and with them we will be in full fellowship. This grouping will exclude or otherwise discipline churches which endanger the substantial agreement. It will act, toward those within and without, with all the authority of the true church. The status of those churches and Christians who do not belong to our grouping is a matter we would rather not be pressed to define; we will not dare say that they are no Christians, yet we cannot admit them to full fellowship because we are not sure of their discipline. This approach has the advantage of conserving an earnest concern for discipleship and disciplined obedience as the base of Christian fellowship. However, the necessity of managing the "grouping of churches in substantial agreement" involves a temptation toward formalism, legalism, and self-righteousness of which the inability to "get across" one's testimony to other Christian groups is a symptom. Such an attitude is sectarian, because it basically questions the validity of the faith of those whom it excludes.

Another solution is that of denominationalism. Not having any especially serious concern for discipleship or discipline, a group of churches bound together by a common past continue to maintain distinct organizations which have no clear reason, except tradition or sentiment, for existence. The denomination differs from the "sect" as described above in that, having no clear discipline, it considers other denominations, held to other sentiments and traditions, as having just as much right to exist. This mutual respect of one denomination for another may be called tolerance, but at the same time it is indifference to questions of truth and ethics, for contradictory positions cannot be equally valid.

If we were obliged to choose between these two possibilities, it is clear that the preference would belong to the former. Yet neither begins with Biblical principle. Both begin with a group of churches, bound together by tradition or conviction, and then ask: do we want discipline? To be thoroughly Biblical we should not accept thus uncritically the prior existence of the group of churches, with the *a priori* decision to exclude whom the group excludes and include whom the group includes.

Paul's reprimand addressed to the Christians at Corinth in chapters 1 and 2 of the first epistle makes it clear that no barrier to Christian fellowship, based on factors either of social sympathy or of doctrinal tendency, is justified which excludes other sincere Christians. This same epistle is categorical about the need for excommunication in cases of unrepentant disobedience; so we know that being serious about discipline is not inconsistent with this broad conception of fellowship. Though the form of its application may vary, and will be hard to determine, we have no reason to suppose that this principle has lost its validity since New Testament times: fellowship with every sincere Christian, exclusion of the unrepentant disobedient. The problem of application arises when many sincere Christians act in ways which look like disobedience. Yet in honesty we must admit that the behavior which appears to be disobedience is not *unrepentant*; its origin is not in a rebellious will but in ignorance, misunderstanding, or variant conviction as to the true path of obedience. When the ignorance has been dispelled by spiritual instruction, we may then raise the question of discipleship, and thus of discipline, in its true light, excluding from fellowship those who obstinately refuse to conform to truth whose validity they cannot deny; but not until then.

The legalist error would be to base a judgment on a rule concerning the act without consideration of the degree of illumination; the pietist error would be to base a judgment on an evaluation of sincerity or piety without considering obedience. Both errors have the same origin; the artificial separation of the act from its spiritual foundation.

It is clear that if there is to be ethical earnestness, there must be clarity of both instruction and discipline in the church. Instruction and discipline may be based not only on indubitable Scriptural commands (such as the condemnation of murder or theft) but also on the adaptations and extensions which the brotherhood, in fidelity to New Testament principle, has been led to consider as necessary for a given time and place. Then the basic question is how the brotherhood arrives at its decisions, both as to the ethical principles and as to their application to individual members.

The New Testament gives us a precedent in its view of the church which provides answers both to the question of discipline and to the question of how we are to understand the "denominational" groupings. The burden of proof lies with those who would claim that the New Testament conception is not applicable. Again we may note, though Mennonite history is not our interest here, that the Mennonites of Switzerland, Alsace, and Lorraine consider this to be the historic Mennonite position.

The Church, as we find the word *ekklesia* used in the New Testament, is first of all the people of God; not an institution but a spiritual fellowship of members who belong to it because each has followed personally a personal call. The Church is not invisible, as it is the unity of tangible Christians; but the doctrine of the invisible church invented by Augustine is valid at least in so far as it negates the identification of the church with an administrative organization. The Church may *have* an administrative organization, or several; but in no case *is* the Church an organization. Not only Catholicism is mistaken at this point.

But if the Church's visibility is not that of an organization, how does this universal spiritual unity take form, make decisions, and act in the world? The New Testament's second usage of the word "Church" is the answer; it refers to the Christians in a given locality, i.e., the congregation. It is in the congregation, assembled under the leadership of the elders, that the promised Spirit manifests His presence and leads in prayer, in exhortation, and in discipline. It is therefore also in the congregation that the "ticklish" questions of discipline, the evaluation of the relation between knowledge and obedience in each individual case, and the consequent decisions as to means of application, can be made. Only a local group is capable of making such a decision, since it involves dealing with unique personalities, not with rules. The same applies to the choice of ministers for similar rules.

The New Testament does not command a congregational polity; it presupposes it. The uses of the word "church" to refer to a denomination (as the Mennonite Church or the National Reformed Church of Geneva) or to a building are unknown in the apostolic writings. There are no warnings against a hierarchical organization because none existed, and even the leadership position of the Jerusalem church was not an effort at hierarchical authority. There are, however, apparent exceptions to the rule of congregational decision which must be mentioned here. One is the case of the apostles who, despite their respect for congregational autonomy, still had great authority. We have seen, however, that this authority has its counterpart for our day not in the ministry nor in church order but in Scripture. Further, this authority concerned chiefly the period of the founding of a church; the apostle's aim was, through the naming of elders, to enable the congregation to function when he left for other fields of evangelization. The case of Timothy or Titus as evangelists and apostolic delegates is similar. The evangelist's authority, nearest to that of the apostle *before* the formation of a local church, is not exercised *within* the existing church, and is thus no exception to the general pattern of congregational decision. The fact that the "pastoral" epistles give instructions to name elders, and not to plan for a succession of apostolic delegates, is a further indication that the evangelist's function, after founding a church, is to become dispensable.

Thirdly, there is the case of the Jerusalem "conference," sometimes cited as a precedent for a "synodical" type of church order. But in reality the report in Acts emphasizes that it was an apostolic meeting, which is an indication that such a meeting was unique, not a precedent. Paul says that its purpose was to obtain the other apostles' ratification of his ministry. The only other kind of authority exercised by the Jerusalem conference was not that of a synod (only three people from outside Jerusalem were present) but that of a congregation (Acts 15 mentions repeatedly the presence of "elders and brethren"), which, due to the presence of the apostles, had the special authority of "mother church." In this sense also, the precedent is unrepeatable, except perhaps in a limited way in the beginning of mission work in a new culture, where the oldest congregation might again have a sort of "mother church" status.

The New Testament principle that the basic unit of decision and action is the congregation, must be kept in mind if we are to find our way through the questions of polity above the congregational level. We must constantly remind ourselves that no organization is or can be the church; even if an organization did succeed in uniting all Christians and excluding all non-Christians, it would not be the church, but only the church's servant. Thus if any agency above the congregational level, be it episcopal, synodical, or ecumenical, attempts to be the Church or act as the Church in defining the conditions of fellowship, that agency is infringing upon the prerogatives of the Church in its local visible form. Yet the problem of interrelating local congregations demands nevertheless all sorts of adjustments which cannot be left to chance or to fortuitous arrangements. What then is the status of conferences, denominations, and interdenominational movements? To answer, we must start from the basic unit, not from our preoccupation with certain current problems of church leadership.

The congregation faces, for one thing, the problem of admitting outsiders, whether passing visitors or people moving into the area, to fellowship. If there is to be a consistent relationship of fellowship to discipleship, the candidate must be examined; asked whether he has been baptized on confession of faith, whether he is committed to discipleship, whether he is at present in vital fellowship with the Lord. If possible the judgment of someone who knows the person should be obtained. (It might be noted that in churches of Open Brethren and Apostolic tendencies, this examination goes on at every meeting before the administration of communion, and the elders announce to the congregation the names of those visitors or newly arrived brethren who will partake.) If, however, it can be known that the visitor is a member in good standing of a congregation whose examination is based on the same criteria, a detailed examination will not be necessary. Thus it is possible for a denominational agency such as a conference, *as long as* the congregations involved are profoundly agreed as to the criteria of discipline, to serve, so to speak, as a sort of clearinghouse for certificates of eligibility for fellowship. If, however, the conference begins to consider itself an enforcement agency for imposing standards upon congregations which are not profoundly agreed, the whole justification collapses.

Secondly, each congregation must continually face new problems and find new solutions to difficulties which, though they must be met on the congregational level, require advice and information from other Christians. The conference or other agency can be the forum for the mutual interchange of such fraternal counsel, such as that sent by the mother church at Jerusalem to the churches of pagan origin. It can be truly a help to congregations facing new problems to benefit from the advice and varied experiences of others; yet at the same time, we must be on guard against the euphemistic use of the term "help" to refer to what is really outside interference in the decision processes of the congregation. Interchange on this level requires of the congregations sufficient in common to be able to discuss profitably, but the unity need not be so profound as for the function of "clearinghouse for fellowship."

Thirdly, each congregation has a responsibility for activities of service and witness which cannot be done locally: missions, relief, publications, education, etc. Co-operative agencies on any level uniting congregations of similar conviction are therefore necessary, and the only criteria to which they are subject are those concerning their faithfulness in reaching the goals set. The degree of doctrinal or disciplinary agreement necessary depends on the work at hand; evangelization, education, or the peace witness require considerable unity; disaster relief, the repression of pornographic literature, or the advocacy of marital faithfulness demand much less.

Fourthly, in the interest of the total Christian witness, no obedient congregation can be complacent about the differences and even contradictions between the doctrinal and ethical positions of the various Christian movements. The fact that the congregation is the basic unit of the Church's visibility is not an argument in favor of disunity, but rather in favor of the true path to unity. God's purpose with His Church, and therefore each congregation's purpose in relation to all the others, is growth toward unity of obedience and fellowship. Unity of organization may be either good or bad depending on whether it aids or hinders the achievement of the obedient unity of congregations. Toward this end there is needed an interchange of advice and exhortation, not only between churches which agree, for help in applying discipline, but also between churches which do not yet agree, for mutual correction and instruction. This may be on an inter-Mennonite level (such as an [Old] Mennonite discussion of dress standards), on a pan-Mennonite level (such as a discussion within the Mennonite Central Committee constituency on the relative importance of various kinds of service work, or such as a Mennonite World Conference), on an "evangelical" level (such as a nonresistant witness to the National Association of Evangelicals), or on a still broader scale (Church Peace Mission, Continuation Committee of the Historic Peace Churches, World Council of Churches). Of course the content of what may fruitfully be discussed will vary on the different levels in proportion to the degree of spiritual agreement between the participants in the interchange, but on every level the obedient church has a witness to her sister churches. No such organization, even on the narrowest purely confessional scale, is legitimate if it usurps the functions of the church. The Federal Council of Churches, for instance, overstepped its bounds in World War I by making a pronouncement in favor of the war, which not all its members supported, and by favoring definitely a certain (liberal) theological position. The Mennonites, who at that time found themselves obliged to withdraw from that organization, were justified. Whether that same "superchurch" tendency still exists in the National Council of Churches is still being debated; but it is largely absent in the World Council of Churches, where our evangelical and nonresistant witness is needed, would be welcomed, and would find points of contact in the new interest in Bible study and the rethinking of social strategies. If we were to judge it as a church, we should of course not join the World Council; but it is not a church, only a servant of the churches. The presence within it of theological liberals, militarists, and pedobaptists would disqualify the W.C.C. as a church, as a clearinghouse for fellowship, and to some extent as an agency for service and witness, but not as a forum for discussion.

Thus we see that the New Testament's "congregationalism" as here understood is not opposed to all activity above the congregational level; it rather assists such activity by showing its clear legitimacy without hardening it into a specific pattern of polity. There can and should be intercongregational collaboration on all levels and with varying purposes, all of them serving to keep us from identifying our organization with the church. The form and size of such agencies and interrelations are matters of purely pragmatic interest, to be determined in terms of the defined goals and the degree of agreement which is necessary in order for those goals to be sought in common. For pragmatic reasons, one will avoid both excessive size, which can lead to loss of the personal touch, bureaucratization, lack of contact with congregations and of feeling for local problems, bureaucratization and inattentiveness to new leading; and excessive smallness, which brings with it duplication of functions, organizational overhead, narrowness of horizon, and limited resources. Those forms which tend to preserve congregational individuality—conference, synod—will in general be preferred to those which lead to thinking of the church as an organization—episcopacy, adventism, Salvation Army. For similar reasons one will prefer a loosely bound series of agencies with prelimited assignments to one tight organization dealing with all of the several concerns listed above.

The purpose of this paper has not been to provide final answers but to ask primary questions, in light of the conviction that Scripture cannot be irrelevant for the details of twentieth-century church life, and that the burden of proof lies with those who would consider the modern church authorized to invent new answers to new questions. If present developments in the Mennonite churches are not clearly guided by the Biblical orientation toward new problems, they might be seen later to be what one student of Anabaptist and Mennonite history has called "new insights which really involved the sacrifice of principle," and the result can only be the ultimate degeneration of the disciplined fellowship into the denomination. Yet on the other hand if the present time of searching and testing can lead to a rediscovery of what Biblicism truly does and does not mean, and a new understanding of the relation of fellowship, discipleship, and discipline, the Mennonite brotherhood has before it the open door to a ministry, in its own right and in witness to the rest of the Church, of imponderable significance, in a historical situation more open to that ministry than ever before in modern times.

APPENDIX
Close Communion—On What Lines?

After the main body of the present paper had been completed, there appeared in the *Gospel Herald* for Jan. 11, 1955, an article entitled "Communion—Close or Open?" by H. S. Bender. It goes without saying that the writers of the present paper are in full agreement with the basic starting point of that article: the contention that communion is the celebration of the unity, not only in worship or commemoration, but also in discipleship, of the Christian fellowship, so that it is unfitting for individuals whose commitment to consistent discipleship is not explicit in word and life. It seems, however, that some of the arguments by which Brother Bender proceeds from this starting point to conclusions as to application of this principle within divided Christendom do not attempt to apply to the denominational problem the attitude toward the church which we have seen in this paper to be that of the New Testament. The question we should like to ask is thus not: "Communion—Close or Open?" but "Close Communion —How?"

In the New Testament we have seen that the basic authority for discipline and also for communion, and the basic unit within which communion expresses itself is the local congregation. Both at Corinth and at Antioch, Paul refused to tolerate the exclusion from fellowship of any Christians, whether on the basis of legalism or of personal loyalties to a leader. Thus the local congregation does not mean a gathering of people who exclude others and unite on the basis of some common sentiment, but rather the total number of Christians in one place. "Denomination" means "naming"; thus the four groups in Corinth (I Cor. 1) who named themselves according to their favored teachers were the first Christian denominations; and Paul does not give us the impression that they are desirable. Only as the unity of all true Christians in the locality can the congregation be a faithful representative and "visualization" of the Church.

Near the beginning of his article, Brother Bender mentions the congregation as a possible level of discussion, but in the rest of the article his thinking consistently follows denominational lines. Strictly speaking, in terms of the question posed in the article's title, this is no handicap, since the whether of close communion could be discussed without asking on what level the judgments as to eligibility are to be made; in reality, however, the article discusses not only the whether of close communion but also the how, and since the general tendency is to favor the denomination as the rule for such decision, we may rightly ask whether such a decision is Biblically justified. The really serious questioning of current Mennonite practice of close communion does not come from those who would like non-Christians or unfaithful Christians to be able to commune—thus the whether of close communion is not in question—but from those who doubt that denominational adhesion is a valid basis for admission or exclusion.

Brother Bender recognizes to some extent the weight of this criticism, in mentioning with approbation the practice of inviting to the communion table nonmembers of "like faith and practice." This is a crucial point in the discussion, for the judgment as to what constitutes "like faith and practice" must be made somewhere. In practice it often means that the individual visitor makes his own decision as to whether he wishes to commune; this means a sacrifice of the whole purpose of close communion, and can hardly be what is meant. Another possible interpretation is that the decision remains on a denominational level: the invitation would then apply to "anyone whose denomination agrees substantially with ours." This is open to the same criticism as was raised in the first place. The third solution would be to make the choice congregational, requesting each visitor who desires to take communion to introduce himself to the elders before the service and make clear the nature of his personal commitment to discipleship. This practice, which is not a novelty in churches of Anabaptist extraction, would appear to the present writers to be the solution nearest the Biblical example; it, however, is not what is generally understood in Mennonite circles as close communion.

Doctrinally the most disquieting thing in the article is the complacency with which the denominational situation is accepted; it is even argued that out of "courtesy" other Christians should not attempt to force their fellowship on Mennonites. Such a "courtesy" which consists in not seeking fellowship would be difficult to justify from the New Testament. The Christian doctrine of the Church as the Body of Christ and communion of saints has here been abandoned for a sociological and pragmatic understanding of the Church as an association of people with similar interests. This makes it possible to think in terms of "our Church" and "their Church" in such a way as to forget that for the New Testament the Church is neither ours nor theirs but Christ's. Granted, Christianity is divided; we must accept that dividedness as a fact; but our starting point in thinking about the Church dare never be our acceptance of that fact as normal or desirable. Our starting point to speak of the Church must be the Biblical doctrine of the Church; from that vantage point we see that the existence of the denomination is subject to serious criticism and in no way normal. Such a complacency as to the denominational situation is really consistent only for a denomination which believes that outside its own organization there are no real Christians—as is believed by the Jehovah's Witnesses and the Roman Catholics. Such an attitude is sectarian in the bad sense of the word. Once, however, we admit there can be Christians outside our denomination, we must find expression for our unity in Christ, as well as means of discussion on those points where we are not united. Such attempts at discussion and fellowship in no way endanger the high view of discipleship which the congregation maintains for those who are the objects of its pastoral responsibility.

Because the denominational situation makes it possible for sincere Christians to disagree among themselves as to the ideal Christian life, we must remember that the only Scriptural ground for exclusion of a Christian is his persistent refusal to repent. There is no clear reason for exclusion based on disagreements where the other person, due to different denominational and spiritual history, is, in sincerity, and in fellowship with Christ, of another opinion. Thus the hypothetical example of a person disciplined for having accepted military service, who would request communion on the basis of his good standing in another denomination, is not to the point, as he is not a person whose dissident position is the result of ignorance of the question or sincere belief in another answer to it. The basic question for the application of close communion is that of the visiting Christian who desires communion and is in good standing with his own congregation, while he is not fully in accord with the communing congregation's position on matters of form or ethics. The sectarian answer would be to exclude him. The New Testament answer would be to consider him as a brother who is not full grown in his faith (and by the way, who of us can say that he is full grown in faith? Yet God accepts us, and so do our brethren), and who needs both our fellowship and our exhortation. Naturally, if such a visitor were to prolong his stay, his status would tend to become that of a member of the local congregation; toward that end there would have to be a process of education and edification which would normally lead either to his coming to substantial agreement or to his no longer desiring continuing communion.

We have already indicated, in the main body of the paper, the several justifications of the denomination. One was its service in maintaining the unity of several congregations with discipline so similar that full fellowship of any member of one congregation in any other congregation is possible without question. This justification of a discipline on denominational lines may, however, not serve to exclude anyone from one congregation who has not been excluded by one of the others; thus the close communion even in such a context does not follow denominational lines; someone not a member of an affiliated congregation may be admitted to communion, but on the basis of an examination which must go into more detail in order to ascertain his readiness. Further, the base of agreement within the denomination or congregation must always be open to deepening and revision. We should be aware of the inconsistency involved when our discipline demands a very precisely defined application of Matt. 5:43 and I Cor. 11:10, at the same time that Matt. 6:19 and Eph. 4:31 hardly ever are clearly a basis for disciplinary measures.

In sum, the traditional Mennonite position is fundamentally right in its insistence that there must be a serious relation between discipline and discipleship in the local congregation, and that this seriousness should rightly be expressed in the administration of communion. It is inadequate only in that, due to a failure to see the denominational problem in the light of the New Testament doctrine of the Church, there has been a tendency for the application of close communion to follow denominational rather than congregational lines.

Now the company of those who believed were of one heart and soul, and no one said that any of the things which he possessed was his own.
—**Acts 4:32, RSV**

God is my witness, that I desire to belong to only one sect, namely the community of saints, wherever it may be found.
—**Hans Denk, (Letter to Oecolampadius, 1527)**

The goal of His purpose is not a collection of individual spirits abstracted one by one from their involvement in the world of matter and in the human community and set in a new and purely spiritual relation to Himself . . . . The redemption with which He is concerned is both social and cosmic, and therefore the way of its working involves at every point the recreation of true human relationships and of true relationship between man and the rest of the created order .
—**Lesslie Newbigin (*The Household of Faith*, Friendship Press, 1954, p. 107)**

VOLUME 3

1956

PREFACE by Paul Peachey

It is well known that Christian movements tend to run in cycles. They begin as creative fellowships but eventually develop into social institutions, conservative rather than prophetic in nature. Where no genuine revitalization occurs, development does not halt at this point, however, but is likely to result in secularization.

Ernst Troeltsch, the great liberal pioneer in the sociology of Christianity, held that an individualistic mysticism tempered by humanism represented the type of religious expression most congenial to man in the modern scientific and technological society. As a description of much of contemporary Protestantism, Troeltsch's view is undoubtedly valid—the impersonal, non-binding, aesthetically stimulating worship service found in many churches in Europe and America is eminently suited to the striving individual in the competitive and/or mass society.

But Troeltsch did not live to complete the chapter filled in by recent decades. For these decades, filled with neuroses and social disorganization, have made clear in practice what the New Testament has told us all along—such individualism is not truly the church which is the body of Christ. The distressing thing, however, is to note that within existing "churches," modern man all too seldom finds the alternative to such individualism. All too often the "churches" can only offer him instead an ecclesiastical structure—an institution to obey or to rely upon. In either event, the modern inquirer does not truly encounter the church. And so modern man languishes between the alternatives of structure and individualism. The former may indeed embrace the true theology of atonement. The latter appeals by its apparent freedom. But neither fulfills the deep human need for redemption in community.

Two articles in this issue of *Concern* are devoted to this question. In the first, John W. Miller and C. Norman Kraus discuss "intimations" of the other way here suggested. In the second, Hans Wiehler examines the place of preaching in the life of the church. Other items include reports from a *Concern* retreat held in late August 1955, and an excerpt from the new Quaker quarterly, *The Call*.

The response to *Concern* so far has been gratifying. However, little of the discussion arising about it has taken written form. It is our purpose to make this pamphlet truly a forum, particularly where differences in view are involved. To this end we solicit your participation. Such contributions will be included in future issues.

P. P.

Intimations of Another Way
A Progress Report

C. Norman Kraus and John W. Miller

In the opening article of the first issue of *Concern* Paul Peachey wrote that "The crisis of the West is to be sought in the dilution of Christianity itself rather than in the secularization of culture in general" (see page 25). This was said after an account was made of the failure of two worldviews which have shaped our Western culture, the medieval *corpus christianum* and modern humanism. After setting forth the logic of sectarian ethics in the second article of that same issue of *Concern*, John Howard Yoder concluded in a similar vein: "This sectarian view," he wrote, "corresponds closely with the New Testament teaching, and regains relevance in every period where a rediscovery of committed discipleship leads to persecution. It, however, appears that religious groups dedicated to this ideal have uniformly deformed or abandoned it with the passage of time, being apparently unprepared for toleration and for transmitting their vision to their children. This historical incapacity of the sectarian approach to maintain its immediacy calls for further study" (see page 43). The conclusions of both of these discussions seemed to call for a renewed effort to understand the Biblical church. This effort was undertaken in the second issue of *Concern*. While much more must be done and is being done by qualified scholars toward the rediscovery of the Biblical moorings that should tie down our thinking concerning the nature and form of the church, it is becoming increasingly clear that something other than a lack of scholarship is keeping us from a full realization of the reality of Christ's church in our time. The question inevitably arises then as to where the difficulty lies and how it is to be overcome. In short: Where to from here?

As we face this question a welter of emotions contend within. Always there is an ugly temptation to Pharisaism lurking behind any effort to grapple with the specific steps of renewal. Seldom are we able to keep ourselves from the pretension of saying more than we know. Equally dangerous, however, is the temptation to fear which keeps us from communicating with the utmost sincerity. How often out of anxiety we contend for something less than the highest to which we have committed ourselves! Caught between the temptation to Pharisaism and the temptation to fearful modesty, the easiest way out would seem to be silence.

That we have not taken this way is due in part to an increasing number of signs across Christendom which indicate that what we have felt and seen is no isolated phenomenon. In the light of reports coming in from every tradition of the worldwide church, we have boldness to believe that the "intimations of another way" that have come to us in past months are not simply some private idiosyncrasies. In any case we know assuredly that pessimistic acquiescence to "things as they are" cannot be the will of Christ for us today.

This paper then is simply to record certain "intimations of another way" that have come to us as we have sought for a fuller realization of Christ's intention for His church in our time, What is presented here is not given as a final answer but as a progress report. Certainly it is not as though a map with clear routings to the promised land has been given into the hands of anyone. If we now seek to spell out in some detail what the way is that we sense we should go, it is not as though all is clarity. It seems to be the technique of God that He leads by steps so that all along the way we should depend solely and completely upon Him.

I

The contemporary situation in the church out of which these "intimations" have been born may be described in various ways. If not the most comprehensive failing that can be pointed to, certainly one of the most obvious is the individualistic character of much modern Christianity. It takes no unusual perception to see that the typical American congregation is made up of religious individualists who may or may not be enthusiastic about their Lord and their salvation, but who could hardly be said to have an enthusiasm for community. It is this loose kind of laissez faire Christianity which prompted Franklin Littell to declare that the typical country club Methodist Church is as "state-church" in character as the state churches of Europe ever were. One joins these churches by a confession of faith which may exalt Jesus Christ as risen Lord and Son of God and yet somehow does not with equal seriousness bring the brother into the circle of attention. Not that the brother is forgotten. He is there on Sunday morning at worship time listening to the preached Word. He is there at the midweek social, eating and talking about all that the newspapers say about this and that. And he is there again perhaps at some other occasion when the church goes bowling or visiting or fund raising or any of the hundreds of things that churches do today. But he is seldom there as the brother in Christ, whom to know rightly is indeed to know Christ Himself, and whom not to know at the deepest levels of spiritual sharing and concern is to miss Christ Himself.

We believe that it is precisely here that an "about-face" must take place, and suggest that the theological grounds for such a turning are nowhere more clearly set forth than in Matthew 18. The oft-quoted sentence: "For where two or three are gathered in my name, there am I in the midst of them" (18:20, RSV) transcends much of our commonplace thinking about the church in terms of membership roles, organization, and building. Here as constitutive for His church stands in all simplicity a double reality which at bottom is one: The gathering with the brother in the name of Christ. In a recent study of "The Church In the Bible," Erland Waltner calls this "the clearest and simplest formula for the church in the Bible." Summarizing its significance in his own words, Walther writes: "The church is where Christ is in the midst of His gathered people." The *gathering* in the *name of Christ*—these are the essential elements in the teaching of Christ Himself concerning His church. What a simple yet foundational place is given here to the relationship with the brother!

But not only do Christ's words here point to the fundamental necessity of gathering with the brother as a condition for experiencing the reality of His presence, but they exalt at the same time the potential significance of *every* such gathering. Christ's teachings here seem to suggest that there is no assembly in the name of Christ, whether it be the chance assembly of two or three traveling companions or the periodic gathering of geographically related neighbors, that is not at the same time filled with all the possibilities of the "church." Not necessarily where the membership rolls are kept, not necessarily where the preacher stands Sunday by Sunday to present his twenty- or forty-minute discourse, at least not *only* here is the church, but *wherever* Christ is reigning in the midst of His gathered people. It is worth noting that a similar comprehension was already wrought out in the Old Testament, particularly in the prophetic ministry of that unknown prophet whom we term Malachi. Over against the efforts of his day to locate the people of God in terms of human membership rolls, he asserts the importance of that membership roll which God alone knows, and over against the efforts of the priests to gather all of the people in one place about the Jerusalem cult, he gives testimony to the crucial significance of each man talking to his neighbor (Mal. 3:16).

The utter seriousness with which Christ looked upon this gathering with the brother in His name finds perhaps its most powerful expression in the authority which He relegates to every such assembly for "binding" and "loosing" (Matt. 18:18). Implied in these words is the spiritual power to accept and to reject, to forgive and to discipline. This so-called authority of the "keys" which Jesus gave to Peter according to Matthew 16:19 and to the apostles according to John 20:23 is here given to the church, that is, to every gathering in the name of Christ, even if that gathering includes no more than two or three. Accordingly the responsibility for discipline is given into the hands of *every* Christian disciple, and the ultimate authority for discipline is posited in the assembled praying fellowship of believers, in whose midst Christ is truly present. That such was the practice of the early church is indicated by a number of Scriptures, which suggest the responsibility of the church for the individual (I Thess. 5:11, 15; I Cor. 5:2) as well as the responsibility of the individual for every brother (Gal. 6:1 f.; I John 5:16). Indeed, it would seem from Matthew 18 and these other Scriptures that the highest expression of the church's life in this world lies precisely in this exercise of brotherly concern and care for each other.

The implications of all this for the problem of individualism which we posed above are not far to seek. Jesus of course nowhere gives us a detailed answer to the question which seemingly troubles many in our time as to what form life in the church must take. He simply insists on one thing: That for the work of the Kingdom, two or three must gather together in His name. This is the minimum, that brethren come together in real mutuality and in the consciousness of His presence. In fact it is this truth which Christ seemingly underscores with His teaching about the agreement necessary for effective prayer, which we find in this same context (Matt. 18:19). This word "agree" implies an intimacy of exchange and fellowship about some particular "affair" (Gr. *pragma*) connected with the kingdom of God which has resulted in a unity of mind and conviction. Implied is a "relatedness" of brother to brother in the face of a common problem. Implied as well is a process of "talking it up" (to use Littell's expression), out of which emerges a common sense of Christ's will and a common exposure of that sense of will before the face of God in prayer.

It is worth emphasizing that all through this passage Christ uses as the basis of His teaching the numbers two and three. As He spoke, He had before Him undoubtedly the twelve with perhaps several other faithful followers also listening. In other words, the actual congregation which He gathered about Himself during His earthly ministry was, when compared to the typical gatherings of the church today, relatively small and very much in keeping with the numbers two and three, which He uses as a basis of His teaching. We must therefore seriously face up to the possibility that the "smallness" of the primary gathering about Christ is really demanded by the prerequisite "agreement." The gathering about Christ must take place, if it is to take place in any real sense, in agreement with the brother. The confrontation with Christ must have, in other words, as its counterpart a confrontation with the brother. In fact, there is, as the last judgment scene in Matthew 25 indicates, a sense in which an authentic self-giving encounter with the brother is simultaneously an encounter with Christ, so that it is impossible to separate the two. If this is true, the unrelated, individualistic church member in a typical American Protestant congregation can hardly be thought of as "gathering" about Christ in a typical "church" service. What he may offer up there in the moments of worship may be noble and right, but failing to come in "agreement" with his brother means that he fails also at the fundamental point, the point of authority and power for the work of the Kingdom. While no artificial limitations can be imposed on the "size" of a congregational gathering, we must at least be sensitive to those conditions where the mechanics for reaching agreement on the affairs of the Kingdom no longer function, and a pious, shoulder-shrugging individualism takes over. The gathering about Christ that can no longer offer up to Christ oneness of mind has lost its salt.

By way of underscoring what has been said up to this point, we should note again how strongly all this was felt already in the church of the Old Testament. Even the earliest writing prophet, Amos, saw clearly that the "congregational" gatherings at the gate ceased to meet the approval of God at that point where the unity was broken and the free speech of *all* in the assembly endangered. "They hate him who reproves in the gate . . ." (Amos 5:10, RSV). He cried out against those who by the power of money and land sought to take the administration of righteous judgment out of the hands of the "two and three," that is the congregation as a whole, and to deal it out autocratically. Likewise Amos is bitter against those "prudent" who keep silent in such a time (5:13). The discrepancies between rich and poor within the community of Israel were viewed by the prophets not so much from the humanitarian standpoint as from the standpoint of righteous judgment in the "gate." It is the threat to the equalitarian status of all citizens in the fellowship of righteousness at the gate (5:15), a threat which brings silence and nonparticipation to the poor, that is the disturbing factor. When the body of God's people is rent to that extent that a free and spontaneous process of "talking it up" in the congregational gatherings can no longer take place, there the prophet knows Israel has ceased to be the people of the living God.

II

But again: Where to from here? It is certainly clear from the above that the next steps lie neither in the area of technical reorganization nor in any other easily controlled procedures. Christ rules His church through His Spirit and at bottom all renewal in the church must therefore take place in the realm of the Spirit.

If, however, we dare point at this moment to a direction in which we believe the Spirit is leading us, it is to what might be called "the passion for community." It is the loss of the capacity for stirring up "one another to love and good works" (Heb. 10:24) which has been pointed to in the previous pages of this article, and it is the restoration of that community of joyous sharing, which finds its unique Biblical portrayal in Acts 2:42ff., that we seek. The Spirit works "togetherness." The Spirit creates *koinonia*, a quality of togetherness that is undoubtedly far more real than most contemporary Christians can even imagine, for it is the togetherness of the *habhura* (Aramaic for *koinonia*), which in New Testament times undoubtedly meant a fellowship powerful enough to include within itself a kind of communism of goods. Such at least was the *habhura* of Jesus with His disciples (John 13:29).

The primary thing then is that the Spirit awaken us to the sin of our self-sufficient, independent ways, and stir up within us the love for community. It is of the utmost importance that the local congregation be fully aware of its essential character as a corporate reality, the body of Christ. A lack of this awareness and a willingness through ignorance to be merely a *Sunday Evening Club* or a socio-religious community organization for the promotion of better living is the surest way for it to become something less than it was intended to be. Where there is complacency about this, there cannot be renewal. On the other hand, where the looseness of our fellowship in the church is perceived to be sin, there the Spirit can once more speak and work. A genuine awareness of need is the first step in answer to the question: Where to from here?

As we think more concretely of measures that might lead us out of this need to a new realization of Christ's church, two ways of approach seem open, if indeed they can be thought of as two ways. In the first place, there are existing activities in most congregations which stand in need of renewal. As Wedel has pointed out, for example, a ladies' aid society does not automatically become a "hotbed of Christian charity" by meeting in the church house. This of course could be said of all the other activities including the missionary band. That the solution does not lie primarily in the area of reorganization and technique most would agree. But that it likewise does not lie in the direction of a renewal of individualistic piety fostered in the mass revival has not been so clear. We have far too often taken it for granted that a personal experience of forgiveness and a commitment to the faith and discipline of the church are all that is necessary to vital Christianity. What is really lacking in many cases is not individual piety but an awareness of the real nature and purpose of the church, the body of Christ in which each member is an organic part of every other member. Sunday-school classes, midweek prayer groups, and various other meetings already in existence afford opportunities for a discussion of basic issues.

In the second place, it has become apparent to a number of us that another step toward the renewal of which we have spoken is the adoption of a new type of gathering. Nelson Kauffman, in a recent article in the *Gospel Herald*, points in the direction that we have in mind when he writes, "In every community we need Christian men who have a holy dissatisfaction with the *status quo*. These should begin to gather a small number of persons into their homes for discussion of the way of the cross in various human relations, of the meaning of the priesthood of all believers, and of the Christian answer to current problems and for developing plans for disciplined action. These groups will become powerful, pervasive, and dynamically evangelistic as they are disciplined. They will carry their interest into the weekly prayer meeting and church program. They will enjoy being misunderstood, but will win through love, humility, and personal sacrifice."

A little reflection upon this statement will make it clear that it is not just another "meeting" that is being called for here. The church calendar of any reasonably active Protestant congregation in America is already full and bursting at the seams, and more than a passing interest or need would be necessary to justify adding another activity to it. What is being called for here is a new kind of fellowship. The need for this becomes apparent when it is realized that the vast majority of "church" meetings are of the preaching-lecture type, where the *koinonia* as it has been defined above cannot fully come into its own. Such meetings have their place, but they should not assume the all-absorbing position that they have assumed in the contemporary church. The meeting of Christians should be an expression of their passion for fellowship and lend itself to a deepening, of brotherly love and care for each other. The emphasis in the gathering of Christians in the New Testament falls characteristically upon the word *all*. "For you can *all* prophesy one by one, so that *all* may learn and *all* be encouraged" (I Cor. 14:31, RSV). The typical meeting is one in which each makes his contribution and all are built up. "When you come together, each one has a hymn, a lesson, a revelation, a tongue, or an interpretation. Let all things be done for edification" (I Cor. 14:26, RSV). It is the disappearance of this kind of gathering in the vast majority of congregations that is so disturbing. It is the rediscovery of this quality of glad fellowship and its relocation in the center of our church life that we count one of the most important steps toward the realization of the full power and reality of the church.

How this can be done within the organizational framework of our congregations will vary from place to place. Often within given congregations there are prayer meetings, where the group is smaller and perhaps also more aware of the need, that might provide the nucleus for a rebirth of such a fellowship. Perhaps also a Sunday-school class could develop in this direction. The character of Sunday morning and quite often Sunday evening worship has become by and large so fixed and formalized that the procedures here could be altered only with great difficulty. In many situations, the original step in the direction of a more vital *koinonia* will have to take place, as Nelson Kauffman suggests, independent of the formalized church calendar. Those who feel the need and recognize it as a call of the Spirit will be constrained from time to time to move out as they have opportunity into new, and in part independent, expressions of common life. This may take the form of simple, informal meetings in each other's houses, such as we read about in the Book of Acts. It is undoubtedly not without significance that the early church and the Anabaptist church were predominantly house churches (For the practice in the early church, see Floyd V. Filson, "The Significance of the Early House Churches," *Journal of Biblical Literature*, vol. 58, 1939.) It is in this context of the house where so many of our waking and sleeping hours are spent that the fellowship of the saints can take on its most realistic and personal character. The emergence of such fellowshipping *Hausgemeinden* within our larger congregational units is a goal toward which anyone who senses the need can work.

In case it does become necessary to move forward independent of the formalized church calendar, the group will need to be ready to face realistically the difficulties and pitfalls of such an attempt. Perhaps the first practical difficulty will be to find time for such a gathering. If the experience is to be a vital and central part of the lives of those participating, the group should meet regularly and at least biweekly. It is not enough for the group to plan scattered meetings fitted here and there into an already overcrowded schedule. This will almost inevitably mean that members of such groups will have to reevaluate their other activities if they really take their gathering seriously. Further, such a re-evaluation will of necessity raise the basic question with which the group will sooner or later have to wrestle: What is the relation of the "house gathering" to the larger congregation? Is it to be thought of as a prayer band? A pietistic cell group for mutual exhortation and stimulation? Another activity group with its special project? A study group? An auxiliary of the local congregation which will find its block on the diagram of the local organization along with various Sunday-school fellowship gatherings and the youth groups? Should it be placed on the schedule like the Sunday-school teachers' meeting and the midweek prayer meetings?

It has become our conviction that the group is perhaps all of these things and more. It might well be described in the words of Norman Pittenger.

> It is a group of convinced Christian believers, bound together by a dominant loyalty to the Christian church's faith and its divine purpose, and so conscious of this loyalty that it pervades their life and thought. Such a group of Christians is what every parish or congregation is meant to be: it is, as St. Paul would have said, the church, in Corinth or Athens or Ephesus, in Alameda or Tallahassee or Barre. There is nothing esoteric in the conception; it is, in fact, a way of saying that in each and every place where there is a body of Christians, they must be knit into a strong self-conscious group, aware of their function in the world, ready to give themselves to their task as Christians, and co-operating in every respect so that they may most adequately accomplish the work they are given to do. (Norman Pittenger, *The Historic Faith and a Changing World*, New York, Oxford University Press, 1950, pp. 135, 136)

It needs to be pointed out emphatically that such groups dare not be exclusive or in any way tied to the social stratification. They dare never think of themselves as autonomous or self-sustained units. They should rather nourish the life of the congregation. One might almost say that they should be the life of the congregation. Certainly it will be their fervent prayer that the Spirit will bring to the congregation a new awareness of what it essentially is, and that God will hasten the day when the congregation as a whole will find its life anew in a disciplined fellowship where brother knows brother in a new dimension of sharing and participation in the body of Christ.

A clear realization on the part of the house gathering of this relationship and responsibility will guard the group from the pitfall of becoming an end in itself or a semiautonomous auxiliary of the church such as the various Christian business men's associations which have often actually become a rival of the local congregation for the allegiance of its members. It will keep it from becoming ingrown and introspective. Since the goal of the group is nothing less than the renewal of the congregation, it will be ready to make adaptations to the local situation in which it finds itself. On the other hand, it does not automatically solve the very practical problem of fitting the life of the group into the church calendar. Nor does it indicate a clear answer to the question how such a gathering can maintain its life and discipline without coming into conflict with the formalized pattern at certain points. This is an area where much charity and patience will be necessary, and probably, as Nelson Kauffman suggests, the group will have to be willing to be misunderstood.

The leadership in such a development should be of the simplest kind. As a rule, the father of the home in which the meeting takes place should lead the meeting and provide whatever is needed to maintain order such as Paul speaks of in I Corinthians 14:26ff. The spirit of the gathering should be friendly and open, so that no one will be afraid and therefore unable to offer to the group what the Spirit has given him. Often the problems and cares of the day will naturally become the opening topics for group discussion and concern. A too sharp distinction between what we know as "visiting" and the sharing of mutual insight and admonition is a likely sign that the quality of the gathering is not yet moving on the proper level. Where Christians gather they gather in Christ, and all their conversation should be in reality a sharing in the Spirit. This does not mean that a pious tone must enter into our conversations. In fact, such a tone may point to a superficial imposition of our religion on strange materials. Rather what must be grasped is that the most "secular" affairs of our lives and perhaps those conversations in which we think Christ is least involved are often precisely the conversations in which He is most concerned and most actively at work.

This emphasis upon informality and naturalness should not be construed to mean that no pattern should be developed, but certainly the pattern must emerge from the life and character of the meeting, and the group should feel free to experiment in this area. Perhaps the meeting ought to be thought of as a mutual quest or search for the unity and mind of the Spirit. Here in this gathering the members should become in "concrete actuality" what they are, members of the body of Christ. Here their common life should become a reality. Thus the pattern will likely include informal group singing, sharing in confession and discussion, common prayer and searching of the Scripture, and mutual discipline. Although some thought and care should be taken to keep the discussion moving toward a goal, it should be recognized that the primary goal is not a verbal solution, but an actual meeting and fellowshipping of brothers and sisters in Christ. Following the pattern of the early church, some have found that eating a simple meal together has meaning for the group. And it is to be hoped that the day is not too far distant when that most significant and central symbol of Christ's presence with His fellowshipping disciples, the Lord's Supper, can be made a part of the life of the house gathering without causing offense to the larger congregation.

If we begin to gather once again in this spirit, bringing the whole of our everyday living under the Lordship of Christ, the ongoing answer to the question: Where to from here? will persistently and, dare we suggest, ruthlessly emerge—ruthlessly because it will very soon be seen that areas of our lives that we had hitherto considered our "own business" now turn out to be anything but private. It is disturbing to think what some persons are hiding behind the word "private" in contemporary Christian circles. Is it my "own business" if I spend twenty thousand dollars on a house that is not really needed, when my brother is ground under by debt? Is it my "own business" if I weaken under the pressures of advertisement and materialistic cravings and foolishly sell myself deeper and deeper into financial obligation? As fellowship deepens in the mutual exchange of Spirit-given gifts, it will be seen that such matters are far from private but the concern of all. Certainly that picture of almost reckless redistribution of goods which appears in the opening chapters of Acts should rest heavy on the conscience of Christendom, and point us to a more realistic fellowship not only in the so-called spiritual areas, but in matters of economics as well.

Where such fellowships again emerge, the question will soon arise as to the obligations for evangelization. It is a common experience that where something is found, it must be shared. In fact such a realization of fellowship is the only possible climate for missionary outreach. The *kerygma* always proceeds from a messenger who goes out from and returns to a praying, sharing community. The Christ to which he invites men is no disembodied Spirit but the living head of the body which is His church. "Souls" are therefore not won for some mystical experience with a Christ who is known only in a history book, but they are added to (Acts 3:41) a body of fellowshipping persons. It is possibly for this reason that the missionaries to completely un-evangelized lands of whom we read in the New Testament seldom go alone but usually at least by twos. Even here the church must confront the world not in the form of an individual but of a fellowship.

III

As we look forward to the realization of *koinonia* on the lines suggested above, it is well to remember that we are not alone . In fact, as we have already indicated, the most encouraging evidence that these desires are not simply human and carnal is to be found in the widespread and historically unrelated developments in the same direction across the whole ecumenical church. We have noted the emergence of similar convictions within Quaker circles and now finding expression, among other places, in the periodical *The Call*. George MacCleod's Iona Community is exercising a wide felt impact not only on the Scottish Church but in recent years increasingly here in the States. Perhaps of all these various developments, the most instructive for us in the United States will be the newly founded Bruderhof at Woodcrest, New York. The passion for community about which we have been speaking finds in this new Hutterite development a powerful illustration, and most important of all, it is accompanied as it must be by a zeal for missionary ingathering. That a sense of eschatology and a strong consciousness of the Spirit are also alive in this community is to be expected. It is hoped that a conversation can soon be inaugurated between all these various groups, for the concern is at least as broad as the whole peace church movement, and undoubtedly broader.

Preaching in the Church?

Hans-Joachim Wiehler

To avoid all misunderstandings right at the beginning, it is not *preaching* as such that is called to the forum here, although today's connotation of this term might well need a checkup and comparison with the New Testament idea and method of preaching—but the relationship of the pastor to his congregation. In other words: Does preaching have a place *in our churches*?

Today the terms *pastor* and *preacher* are used almost synonymously. When the average man in the street visualizes the job of a pastor or minister, he almost inevitably sees him gesticulating in the pulpit, preaching sermons to his flock. When a little boy imitates a pastor, what does he do? *Preaching* is commonly regarded as the main business of the pastor or minister. *The pastor is the preacher.*

It is this common notion which is questioned seriously in the following pages: first, on the basis of the New Testament; second, against the background of Anabaptist theology (conception of the church) and history; and third, from the viewpoint of modern psychology and personal experience.

I

To describe the act of communication of God's will and Word through Jesus and the apostles to the people, the New Testament uses basically two terms: *Preaching* (*keryssein*—to cry or proclaim as a herald; *evangelizesthai*—to announce good news, to "evangelize") and *Teaching* (*didaskein*—to teach). Yet these two methods of communication do not seem to be co-terminous in the New Testament. C. H. Dodd points out that,

> The New Testament writers draw a clear distinction between preaching and teaching. The distinction is preserved alike in the Gospels, Acts, Epistles, and Apocalypse, and must be considered characteristic of early Christian usage in general. Teaching (*didaskein*) is in the large majority of cases ethical instruction. . . . Preaching, on the other hand, is the public proclamation of Christianity to the non-Christian world. . . .
>
> The verb "to preach" frequently has for its object "the gospel." Indeed, the connection of ideas is so close that *keryssein* by itself can be used as a virtual equivalent for *evangelizesthal*, 'to evangelize,' or 'to preach the gospel.' It would not be too much to say that wherever '*preaching*' is spoken of, it always carries with it the implication of 'good tidings' proclaimed.
>
> For the early church, then, to preach the Gospel was by no means the same thing as to deliver moral instruction or exhortation. While the church was concerned to hand on the teaching of the Lord, it was not by this that it made converts. It was by the *kerygma*, says Paul, not by the *didache*, that it pleased God to save men." (I Cor. 1:21) (italics added, *The Apostolic Preaching and Its Developments*, pp. 7ff.)

According to Dodd, therefore, *preaching*, the proclamation of the Gospel, is an act done to the unconverted, to non-Christians. It is to them that the Good News of salvation is preached. Believers, therefore, do not need the act of preaching. They, according to the New Testament, are in need of *teaching*, consisting of exhortation, explanation of Scripture, and "the more or less informal discussion of various aspects of Christian life and thought" (Dodd).

Even James D. Smart (in *The Teaching Ministry of the Church*, 1954, pp. 11–23) who, as we shall see, does not wholly agree with Dodd's sharp differentiation between preaching and teaching, maintains that,

> . . . *Preaching* essentially is the proclamation of this Word of God to man in his unbelief. . . . *Teaching* essentially (but not exclusively) addresses itself to the situation of the man who has repented and turned to God. . . ." (italics added)

Preaching, therefore, belongs for the most part to the *evangelist*, who brings the Gospel to the unsaved, to the society outside the church.

Teaching, then, is the profession of the pastor. The pastor, the shepherd of his flock, is not a preacher. In the truly Christian congregation, the pulpit is not the place for preaching, but for teaching.

II

Where, then, does the common notion come from that the pastor is the preacher of his congregation? Our Anabaptist-Mennonite conception of the nature of the church calls for a sharp distinction between the secular society (world), the realm of un-regenerated men—and the church, the realm of the saved, the gathering of the believers. We conceive of the church as the fellowship of the saints. The unbelievers do not belong to the fellowship group.

Now a most outstanding characteristic in the beginning of our church in the sixteenth century was the assembly of the *Bible study fellowship groups*, in Zurich, and all over Western Europe, out of which the Anabaptist movement was born. In these primary groups, consisting of saved people looking for more truth and of earnest seekers on the verge of conversion, *Bible* study and informal *discussion* were central. They were *taught* by the Bible in their search for more truth, in their search for the true church. "They admonished one another" was a typical phrase among them. Effective *teaching* went on here, not *preaching*. Our ministers were called "*Lehrer*" (teachers), not preachers. Out of these Bible study cell-group fellowships (the true believers' church) emerged the mighty preachers, the traveling evangelists, "Hecken- and Winkel*prediger*." They spread the movement. But a fellowship group with a strong *teaching* activity was their home base. Teaching, the up-building of the believers to mature faith and for mission, *happened inside the church*, and consequently preaching was done outside.

Where, however, there exists the territorial or state conception of the church, and the whole society in a given territory, saved and unsaved alike, belong to the church—*preaching* is the necessary function *within the church*. Here the unredeemed are expected to sit among the believers in the congregation, and to them the Gospel must be preached. In the state or mass church, the *preaching* of salvation takes the place of teaching. For the *didache* is not for the unconverted. They are only saved through the proclamation (*kerygma*) of the Gospel. And since the congregation usually meets only on Sunday, there is not much, or any, room left for *teaching*. Thus *preaching* occurs at the expense of *teaching*. *The pastor becomes the preacher*. The believers do not get the right food (teaching), the congregation never reaches full maturity, and there is no outreach, no *preaching* done to the outside by emerging mature Christians.

Why are there so few evangelists and teachers emerging out of our present congregations? Why is the enrollment at our Mennonite seminaries on such a low level and seemingly on the decrease? *Preachers and teachers are not produced by preaching*. The Christians who "by this time . . . ought to be teachers" and preachers remain babes in Christ and eventually "become dull of hearing" (Heb. 5:11–12, RSV).

This seems to be the situation in many contemporary churches. James D. Smart, in the book referred to earlier in this discussion, seeks to justify the contemporary practice of *preaching in the church* with the suggestion that no Christian gathering is without its elements of unbelief:

> We need the *preaching* of the word as Christians, because, no matter how far we have gone in faith, there still remains a root of sin and unbelief in us, a place in each of us into which the humbling, transforming word of the Gospel has not yet come. The preacher who makes the mistake of thinking that the good Christians sitting in the pews before him no longer need to hear the *call to repentance* or the *proclamation* of the nearness of the kingdom of Christ has lost all understanding of both the Gospel itself and of the nature of those to whom he is commissioned to *proclaim* it. *Preaching* addresses itself always to man in the distress of his *separation* from and *rebellion* against God. (p. 20; italics added)

Is Smart right in his demand for a continued call to repentance and conversion even after the initial master commitment and conversion of the sinner—who is thus *transformed into a new creature* (even though still far from perfect) and *a believer* (even though not mature)? Can imperfection and immaturity still be classified as *separation* from and *rebellion* against God—to which state *preaching* must address itself? Does not the writer of the letter to the Hebrews speak to this point?

> Therefore let us leave the elementary doctrines of Christ and go on to maturity, not laying again a foundation of repentance from dead works and of faith toward God. (Heb. 6:1, RSV)

The practice of *preaching within the church* needs, then, a serious re-examination. Does not this practice betray a group as belonging to a certain state church tradition? It would appear that a restoration of a new self-consciousness of ourselves as a believers' church will demand a renewed earnestness in the differentiation in our midst between the *preaching* and the *teaching* ministries.

III

The findings of psychology might lead us still a step further. Although we might be convinced that *preaching*—if defined as the proclamation (*kerygma*) of salvation—has no place inside the believers' church, some may still hold that much of our *teaching* could best be done *in the form of sermonic discourse*. The minister thus becomes a *preaching teacher*. He addresses the whole congregation with his sermon-lecture, which has to speak to every believer's condition, regardless of his stage of development and particular need. In the average Mennonite congregation, there are about 150 to 200 listeners in the audience. Can a sermon-preaching method of teaching—*a mass procedure*—effectively meet the need of every listener in audience? Usually the preaching teacher has to remain in the realm of generalities, in order to touch as many hearts as possible. Every one in the lecture audience, adolescent and adult, is at least to get something. Somehow the truth of the Word of God is supposed to penetrate to the heart of every believer, regardless of his receptivity at that moment. Do we actually believe that God's Word is *magic*?

Now psychology teaches us that a mere dishing out of truth, without knowing whether it actually meets a need and creates response, does not do much good to the listener. Truth can only be received if the receiver is ready for it, if he feels an inner need for it. Only then will he respond positively at all. How can a preaching teacher know and meet the needs of his passively quiet audience? In other words, *a mass teaching situation* (preaching) is usually a very questionable method of teaching. Most frequently the teachable believer will respond much better in *a primary group situation*, where he no longer is a passive listener, expected to swallow whatever is being said and taught, but *takes active part in the discussion*. By his being able to partake in the teaching process, his need is revealed, and has a good chance of being answered. But this will only happen in the *small discussion groups* (the original Bible study fellowships of the sixteenth century); in the big crowd he will be quiet, and his neighbor in the pew too. Hardly will his personal need be answered there. And is there real *fellowship, koinonia*, one bearing the other's burden, one teaching another? In the average church service, with the *formality* of the sermon approach (taken over from the institutional mass church with its cold formality), there is usually a wide chasm between the "preacher" and the congregation—already symbolized by the elevated pulpit and the faraway pews. In an informal group situation, this chasm is bridged over, the relationships become more personal, the fellowship proceeds on a much deeper level, and the *teaching*, geared to the personal need, becomes more dynamic and effective (supreme example: Jesus and His primary group of Twelve).

Now some might insist that our present *Sunday-school* program fulfills this teaching function in the church. Actually, there is some truth in this assertion—at least theoretically. Yet, how *vital* is the Sunday-school program in our churches? Which part of the local gathering of the believers gets the most attention today, the "worship service" with the sermon by the preacher-pastor, or the Sunday school? And what relation does the pastor, the teacher of his flock, usually have to the Sunday school? Do we expect him to "teach" a Sunday-school class after (or before) he preaches the sermon? What type of *fellowship* is there in the average Sunday-school class in our churches? Do people feel free to bring their personal convictions and problems to the open? It seems that our present Sunday-school system does not fulfill the above-asserted function.

After so much is said *against* our current practice of *sermon preaching in the church*, group psychology might also have some arguments *in favor* of a type of *sermonic discourse* (but not preaching of salvation) inside the church. In the pastor's task of feeding and building up the flock of believers there will arise times and occasions when group discussion, Bible study, and personal counseling will prove inadequate over against *a hortatory or edifying or clarifying address* by the pastor to the whole congregation. Yet even here the *pastor* remains the *teacher*, and the *preacher* moves about outside the church door.

Summary

1. The New Testament writers draw a clear *distinction* between preaching and teaching. *Preaching* is by and large the public proclamation of the Gospel of salvation to the non-Christian world. *Teaching* essentially is for the up-building of the believers inside the church. The distinctive and unique function of the *pastor* is *teaching* rather than *preaching*.

2. According to our Anabaptist believers' church concept, *teaching* should have *central* place in the fellowship of the saints. In the territorial and mass churches, *preaching* must stand central because of the unregenerate people inside the congregations. Since we Mennonites today expect our pastors to preach to our congregations, we indicate therewith that we have for all practical purposes surrendered our Anabaptist believers' concept of the church to that of the mass church. The Anabaptist movement spread primarily through the *Bible study fellowship groups* of believers and seekers, and the powerful preachers emerged from them. Preachers and teachers are not produced by *preaching* inside the church.

3. Today's findings in psychology suggest that *the best teaching situation is the primary group relationship*, and not the pulpit-pew institutional approach of the mass churches. Example: Jesus and the Twelve.

Suggestion and Recommendation

1. That the usual Sunday morning (or evening) sermon of the pastor should be converted into an instructive, thought-provoking talk which is then the basis for an immediately following discussion and further Bible study by the congregation (taking the place of the conventional Sunday school).

2. Naturally, not everything has been said here. Further discussion is needed and invited.

A CONCERN Retreat

About twenty persons followed the invitation extended by the publishers of *Concern* to participate in a retreat at Camp Luz near Kidron, Ohio, August 27–29, 1955. As the two following reports indicate, this retreat was devoted to the quest for the renewal of the fellowship church. For the final session, the Mennonite ministers from the surrounding communities were invited to share in the results of the meeting.

Preliminary planning is now underway for another retreat in 1956, to which a general invitation is hereby extended. Persons desiring to participate or to receive information as available should write immediately to John W. Miller, 1407 S. Eighth St., Goshen, Indiana, to be placed on the retreat mailing list. Please include also suggestions for date, place of meeting and matters which you feel this retreat should take up.

CONCERN and Camp Luz by J. Lester Brubaker

For a number of years I believe the Lord was preparing me for the experience of the August *Concern* conference.

The problem of the nature of the church was occupying much of my thinking. As I considered this, it seemed to me that we were becoming more and more "denomination" conscious.

The worldliness in the church was a problem; solving this one seemed hopeless. Attempted discipline by authoritative persons in the church seemed ineffective. In my thinking I was turning toward approving democratic procedures and yet was sure that the adoption of pure democracy would in no way stem the tide of worldliness in the church.

The restlessness of many in the church concerned me, and at times I felt something of kinship with them. At the same time I was convinced that leaving the group would increase problems rather than decrease them. A more spiritual congregation seemed far from assured by such action.

These and many related problems were so big that my concern led only to frustration and hopelessness for neither I nor anyone else seemed able to propose any satisfactory solutions.

The problems are still with me; but through the sharing experience with my concerned brethren at Camp Luz, I have come to a new hopefulness and rest through receiving a sense of direction. Some of the problems will always be with me largely unsolved; others have arisen or will develop. But I have come to see, with contentment, that the Christian way is a constant search after the best expression of the life within the individual and "the body."

More heartily than ever before I believe in the practicality of the believers' church and see it as made up of mutually disciplined members. I believe in a radical Christian discipleship that requires both individual and group commitment. I believe the church is a group of people who submit one to another in love. I believe that through group sharing, worshiping, and praying the "congregation" unitedly "senses" the will of God in all matters of mutual concern.

Such a church, I believe, was the New Testament church, and is the true church to this day. For the conviction deepening and practical guiding I received in August I am grateful to God.

CONCERN and Camp Luz by Sol Yoder

During the last four years, I have had the privilege to live and work in Europe both as a Mennonite Central Committee worker in Germany and the Netherlands and as a student at the University of Amsterdam. This afforded me an opportunity—for which I am sincerely grateful—to look back upon Mennonites in America in reference to what I had observed in Europe, whether among Europeans in general or among Mennonites and other Christians. Especially was this true in the Netherlands, where my work at the international Mennonite center "Heerewegen" brought me into daily contact with our Dutch Mennonite brothers.

One finds a marked difference between the atmosphere surrounding life in Europe and America. In America the dilution from Christian to pagan seems so gradual that one is not certain just what the issues are, or just where the various paths will lead us. In Europe, as a result of the terrible catastrophe which it has experienced firsthand, the issues can be seen more distinctly. The tone of life is more sober and serious, for one finds it difficult to live in superficial optimism and to remain oblivious to the sense of disaster which forms the silent backdrop.

The condition of these times in Europe brings to sharp focus the genius of the sixteenth-century Anabaptists—their faithful application of New Testament Christianity in their own period. It brings also the discovery that our American Mennonite tradition is not the one of the Bible. In the Introduction of the first *Concern* pamphlet, the writer points to this failure: ". . . We were unable to define or to communicate the message that seemed implicit in our professed position . . . What we in effect proclaimed as an answer for people in devastated countries (to wit: the 'gathered' pattern of Christian community) was no longer a dynamic transforming leaven in our own midst" (see page 2).

While I was in America, I too had been inspired by reading *The Anabaptist Vision*. But do we not feel a deep disappointment at the lack in our fulfillment of it? Yet, where are these issues being discussed? True, criticism does often sound heartless, especially in view of the sincere, dedicated Christians who are working in our brotherhood. Criticism, too, does often hurt feelings. Would it be best to accept the brotherhood as it is and try to work individually to improve it as we can?

※

My first opportunity to attend one of the annual meetings of the *Concern* group in Europe was an occasion of great joy and liberation. Joy—because we need not, indeed, we may not, be satisfied with anything less than the New Testament church; that we can and must appropriate the same goal as the early Anabaptists had. Liberation—because we are not alone, but have the strength of the brothers united in common faith and obedience to our Lord. We are convinced that the Holy Spirit called us together, that He by His grace dwelt among us to lead, teach, and convict us.

Two words can describe the meeting of Concern at Camp Luz: "Need" and "Search."

We came together because we were driven together by the sense of our need and impoverishment. "Those who are well have no need of a physician, but those who are sick" (Matt. 9:12, RSV). Are we concerned to see how sick we really are? When we analyze our involvement and conformity in economic life, the ground begins to shake and give way under our feet—we feel the need for a Saviour! In our anguish of soul and existentially felt need, we know we are too weak to stand alone: This is the basis for our fellowship. One brother remarked that he had found real fellowship only in two situations during his life, neither of them in the church: One was while in the German army; on the Russian front, he was part of a surrounded detail engaged in a struggle meaning life or death; the second while working as a coal miner sharing the common danger and never knowing who would not return alive to the ground level. Do we realize that this is exactly the situation of Christians too in our times?

"Search" characterized our meetings. Our fellowship based on the sensing of our great need, we engaged in a search for the leading of Jesus Christ as the Lord of His church.

But how could we deal with our concerns, with the issues, until we had first dealt with ourselves? Therefore, we felt the need for a meeting of testimony and confession. We were amazed to realize in what exclusively individualistic terms we had hitherto felt the Spirit working in our lives. Now we discovered the church gathering about. Jesus Christ, the center of our hope and confession; assembled around the written Word for instruction; praying to the Holy Spirit for His guidance and blessing; exhorting and admonishing—even rebuking—the brothers as we shared our concerns with full confidence and fellowship in our common commitment to the Lordship of Christ over our lives; coming even to the point where confession is natural, where one need have no fear to be open and honest; submitting to one another, "in honour preferring one another" (Rom. 12:10); participating in the self-determination of the group and voluntarily accepting its discipline as the truth emerges in the consensus of the group; finding strength in the group fellowship to commit oneself to this truth and obey it as loyal servants of the Lord, to be prepared to go every bit as far as the Spirit leads; and singing together the praises of our Lord who has fulfilled His promise: "For where two or three are gathered in my name, there I am in the midst of them" (Matt. 18:20, RSV; see Matt. 18:15–20).

Thus we discovered the visible church of Christ as the "believer's church," as the "gathered church," where God's own people move in the society of the kingdom of God, where the sharpest cleavage exists between the church and the world, where the boundaries between the two are very distinct in the concrete sociological situation. It is only such a redeemed community which can become a vehicle in the redemptive work of God. It is in such a church—now assembling, now going out into the world—where every Christian is a missionary. It is to such a church that non-Christians can be brought as to the presence of Christ; and where they may be moved to exclaim, as happened in the church of the New Testament: "Behold, the Lord is here!" This is the fellowship and discipline which the Apostle Paul is talking about in his letters.

This group experience at Camp Luz meant more to us than the specific answers we arrived at. We discovered not a *goal*, but a *way*—a creative way to deal with all the problems we feel the need of sharing; we discovered the genius of Christian living in community. It is our conviction that in this small church-unit of primary face-to-face relations, where intimate fellowship and close brotherly contact is possible, here the church of Christ is present in all its glory and power. Here we can seek together what is the heart of our faith and commitment to the Biblical way.

"Where is the disciplined church?" we ask. Not discipline for its own sake, but for the sake of obedience. The consensus emerged from our group that we dare not go back to our former individualism, for to face the issues we are simply too weak to stand alone. Individualism does not give the fullness of Christian experience. We need a disciplined brotherhood church. What we experienced here must be our usual church experience; we must be able to sense the Holy Spirit working in this way as the normal thing.

Although fellowship is certainly possible at a conference of the saints, such as the Camp Luz meeting, this is not the church. The church is the constant unit which meets again and again to carry on mutual discipline; this is the unit where authority rests. It is alarming to note that most of our congregations are simply too big in size to permit the possibility of practicing redemptive discipline as in Matthew 18:15–17. Such a congregation is not the "gathered church." The chief reason why we are not successful in dealing redemptively with disobedient, lukewarm members is that they are not tied to such a church-unit fellowship which can nail them down to commitment to the truth in the case of disobedience to better insight, or which can carry on a sustaining, teaching ministry to make hearts open for the testimony of the Spirit.

Such a unit church dare not become a pietistic cell where one eats the desserts of Christian living but does not do the dirty dishwashing; it dare not enjoy the fellowship of sitting at the feet of Jesus but not carry on mutual discipline. The unit church dare not accept resignedly the co-existence of a false church, but must witness to it and affirm for itself the celebration of the sacraments—baptism and the Lord's Supper.

In our fellowship together, we have sensed definite shortcomings on our part. How we lack a pure heart to really desire fellowship when it strikes too closely at our false fronts or superficial lives! How we shy away from fellowship when it threatens our own ego! How we are reluctant to let the group spell out too clearly specific issues in our compromised lives! How we fight within ourselves against commitment to the truth or conviction which has emerged by the working of the Holy Spirit! Its implications for our brotherhood or families fill us at times with fear and trembling; for we do not see the way clearly where this will lead us. Yet these insights call for immediate commitment. We must commit ourselves like Abraham, who wandered out to an unknown country; it becomes a constant wandering, for at every point Christ's demands confront us to take a further step. "There is no fear in love; but perfect love casteth out fear" (I John 4:18).

We have committed ourselves to carry our concerns to the local congregations. The degree to which we succeed in interpreting our message depends on the degree we have Christ in us. We do not claim that we are better Christians—more loving, more humble. We come only as brothers in need, to seek Christ in our brother as we partake in a group committing itself to the group experience. It is our conviction that in every local congregation, there are at least a few who will find here an answer to their own yearnings, and will recognize the call of the Holy Spirit to fellowship. "And his gifts were that some should be apostles, some prophets, some evangelists, some pastors and teachers, for the equipment of the saints, for the work of ministry, for building up the body of Christ, until we all attain to the unity of the faith and of the knowledge of the Son of God, to mature manhood, to the measure of the stature of the fullness of Christ" (Eph. 4:11–13, RSV).

The Call
Journal of Spiritual Reformation[1]

Lewis Benson

The Society of Friends stands today at the edge of a new era. There is a stirring and a shaking. Old things are crumbling and new things are waiting to appear.

In the midst of differences that have separated us, especially in America, is beginning to flow a unifying current of mutual love and desire to be members one of another "in that Life that changeth not." Dimly in a far corner of our collective awareness begins to shine the light of a conviction that we are, after all, "a people" with a common history of relationship to God.

It is an historic moment, in which the dawn of a new and vital sense of the Quaker message and purpose can release untold measures of healing life and power into the world.

---

1. Publisher's note: the following editor's note preceded Benson's article on *The Call*: A NEW QUAKER QUARTERLY:
Since the publication of *Concern* No. 1 we have been much inspired to learn of an increasing number of groups within varying traditions who are striving toward a rebirth of the church as the gathered people of God. The Holy Spirit is truly at work, today as in earlier times, speaking to the deepest need of the age. We are happy, therefore, to present here, by permission, an excerpt from *The Call*, a new Quaker quarterly. This article, from the pen of Lewis Benson of Philadelphia, is an enlightening illustration of such renewal. *The Call*, beginning in the autumn of 1954, has now appeared five times. The subscription price is $1.50 per year. Address communications to *The Call*, Cope House, Awbury Park, Philadelphia 38, PA.

What is this message and what is this purpose which is peculiarly ours as Quakers?

The Quaker message calls all people everywhere to come, see and taste of a marvelous light and power that God universally provides for the purifying of human life.

God gathered us 300 years ago to be witnesses to the reality of His power to give wholeness and perfectness not only to individual lives but also to the social unity, the group.

God gathered us to be a community of witnesses to stand together before the kingdoms of this world, faithfully testifying to the living presence of the Lord Jesus Christ as an all-sufficient guide for the right ordering of human life—in God's sight.

God gathered us to carry forward *in demonstration* the life of spiritual reformation toward which the Protestant reformers of the 16th century pointed the way, but into which it remained for George Fox and his friends to enter and take possession with the fullness of God's own purpose.

From this purpose, this demonstration, this witnessing, we have long wandered. But now, dear Friends, we are being called back into it. "Today if ye will hear his voice, harden not your hearts." We are being called by God to re-enter the land of our inheritance and to take up again that vocation which He has ordained for us.

"But you are a chosen race, a royal priesthood, a holy nation, God's own people, that you may declare the wonderful deeds of him who called you out of darkness into his marvelous light. Once you were no people but now you are God's people; once you had not received mercy but now you have received mercy" (I Pet. 2:9–10, RSV).

It is with a compelling sense of this time of call and reformation which is upon the Quaker movement that we, the publishers of this little journal (all of us being members of the Society of Friends), feel urged to launch forth with it. Its appearance is small, perhaps even feeble; and as we begin we have no sight of what may be the extent or ending of it. But behind the work is a single and unwavering desire, which we all do own—to show forth in terms of modern life the praises of Him who hath called us out of darkness into His marvelous light.

With *The Call* we raise a standard around which may gather the company of those whose hearts are secretly tendered to see that God does indeed want a people for Himself, even in this evil day and generation—and who long to find one another in the fellowship of such a community.

What Is Spiritual Reformation?

The spiritual reformation rests on two great affirmations:

1. The living Christ is able to instruct the mind of faith in the principles of God's righteousness. The inward assurance and moral certainty that is born of this faith is the Christian's greatest resource for combating the evil in himself and in the world.

2. God wants His people to be gathered into a community of witnesses who by corporate faithfulness to the Word of their Lord bear a joint testimony to His Truth and against the world's evil. The church of the spiritual reformation is able to offer the possibility of participation in such a community.

Today, as in the days of George Fox, these two foundation principles of the spiritual reformation are either ignored or expressly denied in certain Protestant practice. Both Protestant "modernism" and "neo-orthodoxy" are clearly lacking in an appreciation of these basic truths.

Turning to present-day Quakerism, we find that its central principle has been an affirmation about the nature of man, and not an affirmation about Christ and how He informs the conscience and gathers a witnessing community to His power. In short, Friends have not retained the message and mission of the original Quaker spiritual reformers.

Yet, we are convinced that there are still seeds of redemption within the Society of Friends and that God has not turned away nor excused us from bearing before the world the standard of His Truth—not simply as individuals but as a community.

Both "modern" Quakerism and "modern" Protestantism grew out of the same historical situation—the intellectual crisis of the late nineteenth century precipitated by the controversy about science and religion. The literature of modern Quakerism is read with approval by many Protestants, while modern Protestantism appeals to many contemporary Friends.

Both modern Quakerism and Protestantism made too many concessions to the intellectualism and rationalism of that time, concessions which have blunted the edge of the Christian message and tended to equate the dynamic of Christianity with human good will. The historical situation has changed in almost every way in the past seventy years, and the times indeed call for a faith that challenges the standards of the world and generates moral power to combat the evil in the world.

To meet this need created by the world situation, the Protestants have for some years been working on a solution based on a study of the teachings of the original Protestant reformers. This new movement, often called "neo-orthodoxy," does not aim to restore Protestantism in its sixteenth-century form but to rediscover the dynamics of Reformation Christianity and to apply these dynamics to life today. This Protestant movement has gradually acquired considerable momentum. It has played a significant part in the thinking of the ecumenical movement.

It is not our concern to increase or hasten the impact of neo-orthodoxy on the Society of Friends. But like neo-orthodox Protestants, we seek no slavish copying of the spiritual reformers whose work established our Society. We seek the rediscovery of the bases of spiritual reform and the application of those dynamic principles to the present situation.

The end product of our concern is a gathered community of witnesses whose united testimony demonstrates to the world that Christ's reign is established among His people.

Notes on Books

Considerable literature has appeared in recent years dealing with the problems discussed in *Concern*. A few significant titles are listed here, which in one way or another seem relevant. No attempt is made here to evaluate their contents. Naturally they represent a variety of viewpoints.

Christianity and History. By Herbert Butterfield. London: G. Bell and Sons, Ltd., 1950. Pp. 146.
This is a stimulating evaluation of the place of Christianity in western history by an outstanding modern historian (professor at Cambridge University). Butterfield senses the disaster of a Christianity too closely tied to a given culture.

The Household of God. By Lesslie Newbigin. New York: Friendship Press, 1953. Pp. 178.
This remarkable volume by a bishop of the Church of South India comes to grips with basic issues in problems of Christian unity and renewal. The author reveals a deep and sympathetic understanding of the several traditions of church order. Of particular significance is his Chapter 4 on: The Community of the Holy Spirit.

The Misunderstanding of the Church. By Emil Brunner. Tr. by Harold Knight. London: Lutterworth Press, 1952. Pp. 132.
In this volume the well-known Swiss theologian Brunner treats the tension between community and institution in the Christian Church. It is a book, he tells his students, that he did not want to write and yet finally was inwardly driven to do so. Many churchmen have disagreed with his conclusions, but the problems which he raises cannot be evaded.

The Biblical Doctrine of Man in Society. By G. Ernest Wright. London: SCM Press, 1954. Pp. 176.

This volume is the fruit of an ecumenical study group of Chicago theologians but written by a single author who himself participated. Outstanding in this study is the attempt to recover the Hebrew perspective in our understanding of man and the recognition of the central role of community in the scheme of redemption.

Encounter with Revolution. By M. Richard Shaull. New York: Association Press: Association Press, 1955. Pp. 145.

Richard Shaull, currently serving as professor of Church History in the Presbyterian Theological Seminary of Campinas, Brazil, writes in this book with unusual forcefulness and clarity concerning the social revolution that is rocking the world around us. Especially provocative are his concrete suggestions in Part Two directed to the American Christian community.

The Strangeness of the Church. By Daniel Jenkins. New York: Doubleday, 1955.

Daniel Jenkins, an English Congregationalist, discusses in this his latest book the nature, function, and ultimate hope of the church. The first chapters deal with the Biblical concept, and from there the author goes on to a discussion of church polity and the place of the church in the world. Theologically the author stands in the Neo-Calvinist tradition and consequently offers some points of view that are not in accord with the Anabaptist concept of the church. Nevertheless the book is stimulating and worthwhile.

The Historic Faith in a Changing World. By W. Norman Pittenger. New York: Oxford University Press, 1950.

Pittenger, an Episcopalian, surveys the changing American cultural and political scene and suggests the outlines of a relevant Christianity for the new society. Chapter 5, "The Emergence of a New Society," and Chapter 6, "The Church in the New Society," will be of especial interest and challenge to all those who are seeking God's will for the church in our day.

The realities of modern warfare have changed the content of almost every course (at West Point). In hygiene, for example, cadets learn self-aid rather than first aid (there may not be other people around after an atomic blast).
—*Newsweek* **(June 10, 1957, p. 110)**

We have turned every one to his own way.
—Isaiah 53:6

It is to the people of God, Israel and the Church, that the Bible gives its primary attention, rather than to individuals as such.... Individual and community are held together in a viable relationship without either being lost in concentration upon the other.
—G. Ernest Wright (*The Biblical Doctrine of Man in Society*, p. 18)

The grave guilt of those who have called themselves Christians is that they have restricted Christianity to the subjective question of the solitary redemption of the individual. ... There is no reconciliation with God without reconciliation with all men.
—Eberhard Arnold

God ... did visit the Gentiles, to take out of them a people for his name.
—James (Acts 15:14)

VOLUME 4

1957

PREFACE by Paul Peachey

Numerous inquiries have come in recent months regarding more precise formulations of the views represented by the *Concern* pamphlets. On this we have hesitated. On the one hand, the request is not only legitimate but also necessary. A "sure word of prophecy" can be the only adequate basis for faith and life in the Christian community. Nevertheless we have hesitated. For the wrong use of "definitive" formulations is one of the things that many Christians must unlearn today. The creed is there as a means to witness, but it is not the reality of life in Christ. And even when the creed is properly understood, we may still be tempted to hide behind it, to use it as a substitute for our own decision and commitment.

In this issue we make an attempt to answer this request. It comes in the form, first of excerpts of correspondence among those initially engaged in the *Concern* discussions, and then in two papers presenting in different ways the basic concerns at stake. The first paper, by Paul Peachey, was presented to a meeting of the Bible faculties of three Mennonite colleges

(Hesston, Goshen, Eastern Mennonite) in May 1957. The second, by John Howard Yoder, was presented at a retreat held in Versailles, France, in the spring of 1955. As the author points out, this essay may be slightly out of date in some points, but it can well be regarded as the most comprehensive summary of the views represented in this series.

The additional items in this issue continue the discussion on two of the very basic issues which have arisen in the context of this publication, namely the outward organization of the church and the problem of property. A further feature is a few letters of a critically constructive nature. These we received gratefully and will be happy to continue the discussion.

P. P.

Epistolary
An Exchange by Letter

Among Ourselves:

Dear Colleagues,

... Last week John Miller mentioned the need for us in our generation to face together some problems arising in advanced theological study and related fields. With this many ... in Europe now who are or have been studying here, I'm wondering whether we couldn't with profit combine a roundtable discussion of our own with the proposed history course ... (PP,[1] 1951). It would be most important for American Mennonite graduate students in Europe to get together and compare and share ideas and convictions—important not only for our, specific fields ... but also for the general understanding and promotion of our witness outreach. (IBH). The assigning of one day to an "Anabaptist" theme looks to me somewhat questionable. ... I would suggest the more objective and descriptive title of "A Social Strategy for Christians," or something of the sort ... (JHY). Enclosed please find the final draft of the program for our week in Amsterdam. ... The purpose of the program as it now stands is to examine our position in the culture and civilization of our time, as it affects our mission and witness ... (PP, 1952).

... I have a sheaf of letters which arrived following our Amsterdam conference which perpetuate some of our mutual concerns and on which I

---

1. The following persons, with initials following, participated in the original discussions: Irvin B. Horst (IBH); John W. Miller (JWM); Paul Peachey (PP); Calvin Redekop (CR); David A. Shank (DAS); A. Orley Swartzentruber (AOS); and John Howard Yoder (JHY).

wish to offer a few comments. . . It is clear that Amsterdam was not just another conference—at least not for me. Certain things have fastened on to my convictions: (1) that the bright child of neo-anabaptism is not adequate—is impotent to make new Anabaptists; but that we need to be thankful to those who have husbanded and nurtured the child and not throw the baby out with the bath water. (2) Neo-anabaptism is chiefly academic, an interesting subject to build libraries, journals, lectures around—but not to adopt personally in our daily lives . . . (IBH).

This is a letter to us all, aimed to summarize the situation relative to our proposed Easter conference of this year (1953). . . . Anabaptism and Eschatology . . . Old Testament and Eschatology—Miller; Eschatological Content of *Martyrs' Mirror*—Swartzentruber . . . Eschatological Content of Discipleship—Yoder. . . . I have favored Zurich because of the possibilities for outside speakers there . . . (DAS). One of our group writes, "The kind of group we have can easily become sophisticated, smug and even proud. I trust we will be humble and simple in our Zurich conference and open to the Spirit's leading." My own word, in this connection, is that the Lord spoke to us at Amsterdam, and spoke quite loudly. His speaking to us at Zurich depends upon our own willingness to accept the call and commitments that were thrust upon us just nine months ago. May God help us all. (DAS). John Miller has kindly prepared a list of current eschatological literature (enclosed). This will be particularly relevant to the Thursday evening topic which Prof. Brunner has agreed to take. It is a real accommodation that he is coming at all because of his preparations for Japan . . . (PP).

What do you think about my bringing a proposal about publishing a small booklet containing some materials from the Amsterdam seminar and possibly also something from this one? . . . (IBH).

It seems evident . . . that Zurich was not just another bull session. We are all caught in the complexities of our own backgrounds and personalities—and possibly the Spirit has not yet broken through in the sense of all-pervading urgency, but it is clear that we are closer together in spirit and conviction than was the case at Amsterdam . . . (IBH). Following the brief conversation we had in Zurich about the general topic for Brussels, 1954, my impression was that we were vaguely agreed to make the general subject Biblical Theology. . . . Perhaps we are too content to operate with the categories of the received systematic theology. But we agree that the Anabaptist Vision requires some less conventional, more Biblical formulations of such staple doctrines as trinity, atonement, . . . (AOS).

From now until August 1 (1953), when all manuscripts will be in Irvin's hands, the book is our first responsibility, of course . . . (AOS). I myself have not yet turned in my manuscript for the publication—mostly due to pressure of activities—and partly also perhaps due to lack of overwhelming conviction. Working on my paper . . . I began to ask myself a number of questions . . . and I have come to the personal conclusion that the fact that we ourselves are doing the publishing already invalidates the naturalness and naivete that is necessary for a message to be prophetic. . . This in addition to the fact that existing channels for the publishing of such articles are open puts the dot under the question mark . . . (DAS). I got the impression that we felt that the value of what we had to offer resided in the fact that all the different problems were discussed at the same meeting. . . . I believe we . . . wanted to bring these things to bear on our own usefulness more than on the world crisis, and the publication was intended to share, and elicit responses . . . (AOS). I can enter fully into all the hesitance that has been expressed about our booklet, particularly since I've had some months of other work in some of the areas my own papers touch upon and I realize how terribly provisional they are. Indeed, only one conviction is stronger, after having been home a bit, and that is, . . . we must proceed with our plans . . . (PP).

The Amsterdam Club's book seems to be bogging down seriously. I'm therefore making to you a suggestion which Shank would support. . . . Recommend to *MQR* such material as belongs there . . . the rest in a pamphlet series named *Concern* (Dave's suggestion) . . . printing at Scottdale . . but published in the name of the fellowship . . . (JHY, December 1953). This morning I received a card from John Howard casting his vote for publication but in a different form and suggesting a recount of opinion. This leaves me in a quandary. . . . After reading and working through the Ms . . . I was again convinced that it has at least a word of earnest and sincere conviction for the hour. . . . For me there is no more presumption to speak with the written word than with the oral. . . . We dare not fail to pass on what has come to us outside ourselves, even though it is surely mingled with human chaff . . . (IBH). Upon further thought it seems better to me too that publication has been held up, although I was inclined to feel rather frustrated. . . . I agree to publication at Scottdale of our testimonies. . . . Further that our concern continue to find a channel through a series or an irregularly published journal . . . (IBH).

I found the bundle of correspondence very stimulating and refreshing. . . . An excerpt from a letter I received yesterday from a young diploma-ed pastor follows: "I have just been called to a church . . . I see some of the dangers of both extremes vividly portrayed here, and I believe I can understand the problem, but I do not have a realistic solution to a very real problem. . . . Personally, with my head or theoretically, I believe in the radical sect-type church, but in the visible practice of this in our Mennonite Church, we are going to have to face some problems realistically, or else be ecclesiastically schizophrenic. I am concerned about what seems to be a changing conception of the nature of the church within our community." To me it seems clearer daily that between the old- and new-style ecclesiastical structures in our brotherhood now, on the one hand, and the libertinistic individualism that aims at assimilation on the other, some dynamic and creative forces must be released, and that right soon . . . (PP, 1954).

There exists in the American OM [Old Mennonite] church a significant group of younger men devoted to what we could call a "corpus christianum" concept of churchmanship, who feel that it is we who bite the hand that feeds us when we disagree with some modern tendencies of church leadership. They feel, and sincerely, that this approach is historic Mennonitism, in spite of the "new insights" it involves . . . the line of their thought goes back through Horsch to Twisck and the stern side of Menno, whereas we'd rather go farther back to the spiritual side of Sattler. All of which confirms the thesis of my historical essay . . . that an effort whose deep nature is to complete cultural assimilation and accept the reformers' way of using means which contradict the end in the interest of group survival as an organization, sees itself as carrying on, and in fact reviving, the original Anabaptist vision . . . (JHY, 1954).

We do not want to be sectarian. This is a complicated and hard thing to express, but it is all important to me . . . an intensive effort to define the tangible expression of our Christian Gospel can result in arrogancy, and finally an effort to standardize and impose it on others, thus ending exactly where we started, namely, a formalized code. Almost facetiously I say the Mennonites are over-sected . . . (CR, 1954).

First of the things we learned about the Anabaptist movement is that it was more spiritual in character and congregational in polity than our American churches. We discovered that Anabaptist Biblicism was a far cry from the Biblicism of Daniel Kauffman, and were startled, two years ago, to learn that the presuppositions of a historian like John Horsch were so strong as to prevent him from interpreting fairly Dutch Anabaptist history. It is hard to formulate the positive side of this negative criticism in concrete terms, how the American churches would be differently organized if they were more "pneumatic"; the growth of conference and other machinery is not bad in itself but it's poor substitute for the Spirit. (JHY).

Concern stands for a methodological renewal, as Redekop says. And our "method" is just Biblicism, which means that we strive to resemble increasingly the image of God which we see in Christ and in the New Testament's description of the body of Christ . . . (AOS). Further, on the question of authority, particularly in regard to the Reformation to which JHY's remarks about mine are directed: English Anabaptism during the 1535–1558 period, at least, was essentially Hoffmanite, therefore spiritualistic. In England, however, it never led to the Munster aberration and Quakerism became the direct heir of the English variety of the movement. . . . Thus when Friedmann, for example, finds in Quakerism the purest expression of Anabaptism it is not without historical evidence. . . . My own view is that in the earlier phases of the movement there existed an equilibrium between the Inner and the Outer Word which accounted for its insight . . . (IBH). After a careful restudy of Matthew 5 and particularly Matthew 5:17–20 which I did this summer (1954) . . . I am convinced that it is on this basis that Jesus criticized the conception of Biblical authority which the Pharisees had. Matthew 5:18 is the crucial verse. There Christ asserts the authority of the jot and tittle of the Old Testament law in a way that seems at first to reaffirm precisely what the Pharisees had been saying. . . . The verse, however, contains two time clauses . . . which I think are the clue to Christ's thinking here. . . .To that extent in which all is accomplished, the external character of the law loses its force. . . . All of those isolated and external expressions of life as now codified in the law can be understood only in terms of their organic relation to the law of love for God and for man, and insofar as this life of love has become a part of their inner lives by the outpouring of the Spirit, insofar we are no longer bound by the letter of the Old

Testament law. . . . All this is in line with the promise of Jeremiah . . . where he describes the New Covenant as an economy in which the law will be written "within" men "upon their hearts" . . . that is ideally the principle of authority that should obtain in the New Covenant. (JWM). The main burden of this letter is that we haven't finished thrashing around the question of Biblical criticism and its relation to inspiration and discipleship. Studying here (Basel) has made me see clearly how John could get along without an answer and in fact refuse to agree with the rest of us that there is a problem, since there is now a central body of scholarship which, presupposing the whole critical orientation, is rather evangelical in tone. . . . An answer will have to consider at least the following factors: (1) that if you believe in discipleship as we do, the form, also the external form, of Biblical authority means more than if you're satisfied with justification; (2) that if Judeo-Christianity is unique in its history-foundedness, it matters even more that the report should tell the truth . . . ; (3) the answer must be communicable in some way to the ordinary Christian . . . (JHY).

I am eager to relate something of developments here at Goshen in connection with *Concern*. . . . At a certain point in our thinking on these lines (economic problem) . . . we realized that we could go no further until we had discovered each other on a more profound spiritual level. . . . Now John Howard speaks of the Grebel circle which kept coming to the Zurich church. This is what we have discovered: That the Church will not be purified by any overly-zealous prophets preaching at it, but only as we purify ourselves and gather with those so like-minded about Jesus Christ. We believe that the time has come when we must stop talking unless we can be the Church to which we feel led. We can speak to the Church only from an experience of the Church . . . (JWM, September 1955).

I am starting a new round robin, since the old one seems bogged down once more. What I have to say here are mainly reflections that came to me after Bender's visit a few weeks ago. . . . One of the first and most important objections Bender made was to our seeming inability to say what we have to say . . . in such a way that we will give our testimony and yet not arouse the other man's feelings. . . I know this is not what we intend to do, but I ask whether it is not the picture we have given of ourselves. Everybody's question . . . seems to be: What is their intention? . . . (AOS, September 1955). The questions of where next and how to communicate seem to remain the central concern for the moment. The last time I argued that, all communication problems aside, deep differences between us and status quo remain. The continuing struggle confirms this. Nevertheless the general criticism that only a select academic group can find their way with us is valid and one that ought to exercise us most earnestly . . . (PP, December 1955).

Here in America I think it is clear that we have tended in Mennonitism to minimize the significance of the local gathering of believers over against the larger organizational aspects of the Church. I am for a true gathering together of the saints, and I am for it to that extent that nothing else matters until and unless this again happens. The sickness of our institutional life lies not in organization itself, but in the fact that it is not really subservient to the Church-community, that is to the "love community" in its realistic sense of the gathering of the local brotherhood. In fact, as it turns out, the institutions that are meant to promote the kingdom, all too often serve to crush such a true gathering . . . (JWM, August 1956). For the sake of those who have had no contact with us here at Goshen . . . our faith simply stated is that God is seeking a people who will through repentance step out of the old fallen world order into the new life provided for in Christ and regulated and described by His teaching. . . . Whatever the future, I believe that we are firmly committed that our lives shall be given as fully as possible for Christ and the building up of His body, the Church. . . . A good many of us here have been dealing far too long in the realm of thought, and we do not need so much the one mind as the one heart . . . (JWM, December 1956).

Main outside speaker at our meeting this year was a representative of the "No-Church Church." This movement seems to be on the border between a valid de-Constantinization and a dubious movement of Pietism and the Oxford group. I think it well worth our time to converse with them; they are aware of their youth and want to avoid the errors of the West, and someone with four centuries criticizing the West and learning from mistakes should be able to help them . . . (JHY, May 1957).

The Larger Circle:

Kalamazoo, Michigan
March 20, 1956

Dear John,
My warmest approval of the latest number of *Concern*, and many thanks for sending me this issue. . . . I want to congratulate you and the other friends . . . to this very essential undertaking and—if I may call it this way—movement toward the inner renewal of the CHURCH. You have my full-hearted support and agreement in this matter. Needless to say that I read the pamphlet most carefully, and rejoiced in this testimony to a new spirit. . . . Can there be an "ecclesiola in ecclesiam" as the Pietists wanted to achieve? Or is the "Sect-principle" eternal, and bound to produce a sectarian breaking away from the bigger, the "denominational" church? . . . I made this small marginal note in my copy: "Without sharing also in worldly things, i.e., community of goods, no perfect brotherhood can be achieved." The Hutterite way . . . was absolutely consistent, and what the Society of Brothers is doing now . . . is meaningful too. . . . This kind of living is the only safeguard against the "pietist cell," the "ecclesiola in ecclesiam."

Robert Friedmann

Campinas, S.P., Brazil
April 15, 1956

Dear Brother,

Received *Concern* No. 3 in the morning mail . . . in spite of a dozen other things pressing for attention . . . I had to read this from cover to cover. It provokes a lot of thought, stirring up again some dormant ideas, . . . At present I have more questions than answers. That is, I find myself in sympathy with most of what you are saying, but at the same time I feel there is another side to this "nature of the church" thing. . . . I am in a state of reaction against sectarianism. JHY on discipleship was full of overstatement and oversimplification. . . . Dick Shaull here has sympathy with a lot of these ideas, especially on the realization of Christian community, but he blew his top over that article. Seems to me we are still overloaded on the ethical side . . . a needed emphasis in general Christendom, but not for Mennonitism. We need rather a more consistent application of ethic and especially a dose of Gospel. I am not sure if you knew Paul Verghese personally or not—one of the finest Christian spirits I have known. Before he left the U.S. he summed up his experience in this manner: "At Goshen I found new breadth and meaning to the Christian ethic, but I had to go to Princeton to find new insight into the Gospel." Think about this one a while.

Dick Burkholder

※

Goshen, Indiana
October 28, 1954

Dear Brethren of the *Concern*:

This is to thank you for the copy of *Concern* No. 1, which I recently received. I think you are doing a fine job and I wish to encourage the publishing of further numbers. . . . I did notice several expressions in your printed letter [cover letter going with first issue. Ed.], however, which caused my eyebrows to rise a trifle. For example, is the Anabaptist heritage one of "naive Biblicism"? Granted that there is naiveté among us, does it necessarily follow that the Anabaptist heritage is naive? Also, granting that there have been uninformed conference bodies in our history, it would hardly be correct to say that the church high school and the Christian day school movement, and the growing pattern of a trained ministry, are the results of decisions "*made either by one or two leaders or in haste* by uninformed conference bodies." Both of these movements have had a slow but steady growth over a period of years, with much discussion and even debate taking place during these years. . . . This is not to argue for or against either the church high school or the trained ministry (although if I were arguing, I'd be on the affirmative side).

Guy F. Hershberger

※

Alwaye T.C. State, India
January 25, 1956

Dear Brother Irvin,

I so badly wanted to congratulate you on your excellent effort in putting out *Concern*. . . . Much as I would desire to join in the conversation, time bids me wait. . . . Of particular interest to me is the second number on the Church. Being a Catholic (not a Roman one) by conviction, I have to differ from Paul Peachey's keen analysis of Spirit and Form in the Church. The whole problem of the Spirit as opposed to Flesh, and the nature and function of the Holy Spirit are still moot questions in theology. . . . The Spirit as Oneness, as Fullness, and as Wholeness which is Holiness, are aspects which still remain to be examined carefully. The whole eschatological background from which the Church is to be understood is often lacking in many Protestant discussions of the Church. To say that Spirit and response of obedient faith are the marks of the true Church is merely to shelve the problem to a definition of these terms and to the insoluble problem of devising a measuring rod for these two entities.

Paul Verghese

※

(The following excerpts are taken from a report by Paul H. Martin of a *Concern* retreat held at Goshen, Indiana, April 19–20, 1957. This is followed by some comments on the meeting by Lewis Benson, editor of *The Call*, a Quaker Quarterly, Journal of Spiritual Reformation. A fruitful exchange between *The Call* and the *Concern* groups has been going on for some time.   —P.P.)

The Friday afternoon session was opened with a summary of the morning discussion of authority and a conclusion of the extent of agreement between *Concern* and *Call* on the point. . . . The authority is in tradition, the Book, and the Spirit, all three and not one of these. . . . That both groups are willing to take seriously both the historical and the living

Christ . . . was considered a discovery of . . . significance for the *Concern* and *Call* movements.

Then followed a discussion on the relationship of *Concern* and *Call* to the (ethnic) denominational structures of which we are members. Calvin Redekop read a paper in which he gave the term, the Covenant Community, to the total salvation, "A re-creation in which man is reconciled to man, and collectively and individually reconciled to God is what salvation in its fullest sense means." . . . We feel strongly exercised to create this Covenant Community. However . . . problems . . . still face us. . . . What of our relations with fellow Christians? Christ's body is undivided. . . . In the face of growing conviction of the above, any overtly schismatic action is unpardonable. . . .

The somewhat varied response to this paper can be summarized by the following. Before you can say anything to the older brotherhood you must do something. In the quoted words of David Shank, "Let's go out and form new churches and let the new judge the old." . . . But the reply was made that the only way to judge the old is to maintain a connection.

On Friday evening Robert Friedmann introduced a discussion on "The Anabaptist Vision Today." *Gemeinde* instead of church was the Anabaptist word. . . . The Holy Spirit is with the church to make it a *Gemeinde*; otherwise it is an institution. The Anabaptists didn't plan to break away. The Holy Spirit planned it. They had the *charisma* (gift), given of grace by the Holy Spirit. We don't program schism, ever. It comes. It should never be intended on the human level. Break only when the Holy Spirit compels.

On Saturday morning John Miller opened a discussion on the economic pattern of the Covenant Community. He stated that an organ for justice and mutual helpfulness is what we seek. . . . The way requires a radical reordering of our lives though perhaps not giving up of private property. The right way might be different at different places, but the right way at each place must be found.

The rest of Saturday morning and much of the afternoon was given to a presentation and discussion led by Lewis Benson on "The Gospel Order." The new Covenant Community is part of the Gospel itself. It is not a temple worshiping community, but a building of living stones. There is no priestly ministry, nor are there priestly ceremonies. Jesus is the holder of all offices. The church is the community of the holy or obedient.... The minister is simply one called to speak a word God requires to His people.... Christ died that we might have righteousness without legalism and community without institutionalism. It is what has kept Quakers and Mennonites apart for three hundred years.

Concern persons agreed that the spiritual is the reality, but that Christ realized human nature and gave baptism and the Lord's Supper as helps that are needed.... Not to recognize (them) is to contradict the historic Christ, the validity of whose voice was previously affirmed. No grace is mediated by baptism and the Lord's Supper.... Making nonparticipation in these symbols the basis of fellowship is placing something other than Christ at the center of community... (PHM).

Philadelphia, Pennsylvania
April 24, 1957

Dear friends and brethren:
Behind our viewpoint is something that we call "a post Pentecostal prophetic understanding of redemptive history." We feel Anabaptism has always been deficient in this, whereas it has been a conspicuous feature of prophetic Quakerism.... The world is still either Protestant or Catholic. No third kind of Christianity challenges modern man to decision. It is in such a world that our witness is to be launched.... If *Concern* is to be a true resurgence of the original Anabaptist vision, we believe it is bound to realize that there can be no peaceful coexistence between Protestantism and Anabaptism. Anabaptism is not Protestant and is not Catholic. It is a third kind of Christianity in tension with the other two.... To conclude: There seem to be two lines of emphasis in your group. One is concerned for opportunities to live out in a truly brotherly way the implications of the Anabaptist vision within the structure of the existing Mennonite community. The other line of emphasis seems to have more universal implications and seems to be more concerned with a sharp clarification of the essence or true substance of the Anabaptist vision and its re-proclamation in the world today. Hans Wiehler and Norman Kraus both see a trend toward moving in the first direction rather than toward the second, and an actual slackening of the wider vision during the past year.

Is the story of *Call* and *Concern* simply a matter of certain transactions within historical Mennonitism and Quakerism, or is this "the *kairoi* (time) which the Father in His sovereign power has fixed?" Are we they of whom Jesus said, "You shall be my witnesses to the end of the earth," or do we think of ourselves as a minor development in the backwaters of denominational history?

Lewis Benson

What Is CONCERN?

Paul Peachey

The name CONCERN has been given to a pamphlet series dealing with contemporary Christian issues. This designation has also been used loosely with reference to those publishing the series and to their viewpoint. Beyond this, there are many who hold similar views or have been attracted to them. The attempt to avoid precipitous or sectarian action has prevented the formation of a group to which one can belong. Insofar as any coherence obtains among the persons in these categories, the term "movement" might be applied, though even this would probably imply greater strength than actually obtains.

To refer to the publishing group first, it should be noted that all were committed Christians before coming to the "Concern" experience, engaged in and/or preparing for work in various phases of the Mennonite "program." In this situation we shared an insight common to our church workers that there are weaknesses in our churches, but we had been heartened and challenged by "the Anabaptist vision."

What led to the "Concern" conversations, however, was a certain disillusionment with the attempt to revive ethnic Mennonitism by means of a strong denominational and academic program. Not only did the effort apparently fail to halt the deeper acculturation which was going on, but we found ourselves unable to meet the larger problems of witness in our age from the base of (ethnic plus denominational) Mennonitism. We were thus distressed, not as at first, over weaknesses in the denomination—these can be understood—but over the remedy currently applied; not over the great distance we had to cover but over the direction in which we were moving.

This disillusionment threw us back upon ourselves to seek for more adequate spiritual foundation. Various resources came to hand, but more important than any other was our encounter with the sixteenth-century Anabaptists in the documents they themselves produced. What we found in them was not an authoritative doctrine or form normative for all time, but a direct approach to the realities of the faith, remarkably similar to that of first-century Christians.

We should note at this point that we are not alone in raising these questions. They have been raised in a variety of ways in our churches and missions, and especially by our students. It is therefore most urgent that they should be brought up at a meeting of the Bible faculties. So far as our share in conversation is concerned, we are heartened to raise the issue precisely here, because we are among brethren whom we esteem and to whom we are largely indebted for our life and faith. We are here to seek and to share, to testify and to hear testimony. It is in this way that God has ordained that His children should find their way in the world.

As already implied, we find the Christian faith a matter of a living relationship with a living God. It is to this reality that we are committed, and regarding which we make our affirmations. These affirmations are therefore not normative dogmas or propositions, to be regarded in themselves as the essence or locus of truth, but rather testimonies designed to lead to the living reality of "Christ in you, the hope of glory" (Colossians 1:27). We have consistently hesitated, however, to put forth a summary of our witness, lest it be understood as a mere doctrinal debate. On this occasion a kind of summary will be necessary, but we preface it with the caution that the problem is not one of dogma versus dogma.

We accept and affirm the testimony of Scripture that God was in Christ, reconciling the world to Himself (II Corinthians 5:19), and have committed ourselves unreservedly, though in our weakness, to His living lordship. We believe that God in Christ is actively gathering His people, the Church, in the world today, and that this Church is "the fellowship of those who have responded to the call to discipleship" (JHY). We believe that this fellowship means the common life of the children of God which embraces their whole being. It is here and in this sense that the kingdom of God has come.

We find that the Church as the universal people of God becomes actual and visible in the church local, that it is realized in the real presence of Christ in its midst, in the fellowship of forgiveness and obedience, of mutual care and exhortation. It is in this assembly that Christ dwells and rules. It is here (Matthew 18:20) that through the witness of the Spirit and the apostles (John 15:26f.) His will becomes manifest, and His grace flows to all unitedly. It is here that the gifts of the Spirit are distributed, where each as a participant in the common life performs his own ministry. It is here, too, in the sharing from assembly to assembly that the universal life of the Church is expressed.

In this faith we find both affirmation and rejection of this present world—affirmation because this is the sphere of divine creation and of redemption where God is working out His purposes; rejection because here, too, demonic forces are at work and the Kingdom already here hastens to a fulfillment beyond this age, leaving behind that which does not belong to it.

These affirmations, we submit, are nothing new, and believe that we here are all united in them. But we also are deeply aware that as one goes beyond their mere doctrinal meaning to their inner reality, this reality calls into deep question many of the assumptions upon which our denominational life is built. A few examples follow.

1. The rational social organization of the denomination is mistaken for the Church portrayed above. This is evidenced in (a) the lack of reality in much of our stereotyped church life (formal meetings, formal speeches, the church often little more than a mediocre lecture club); (b) the church as a "program" to be run by the few experts (whether centralized pastoral administrations or denominational machines); (c) religious leadership becoming more and more a technical skill for which the young are trained scientifically and rationally, with the disappearance of the charisma; (d) the subordination of vital issues to administrative expediency ("smooth" functioning of the program becomes more important than the truth); (e) the insistence that all spiritual initiative must pass through "official" channels; (f) a worldly belief in progress through ever greater efficiency of operation, an optimism thus blinded to the deeper secularization which is outdistancing the progress; (g) our failure to evangelize despite the great activism.

2. This is closely akin to our acceptance of the denominational character of "Christendom" as a "given," which does not distress us and regarding which we cannot hope for a Biblical answer. This is evidenced in the way that, whatever we say doctrinally, the Church universal for us existentially is the Mennonite Church (it is to it that we refer when we use the term "church" generically). This means, strangely enough, that we cannot accept the church local as in every sense the Church, and yet we ascribe to the denomination the sovereign attributes of the Church universal. It means that when we speak of loyalty to Christ or of revival, we rarely assume that either loyalty or revival might bring this state of affairs into judgment.

3. It is increasingly evident that in spite of our progress (we do not deny that there has been some), our prophetic relationship to the "world" is becoming less clear. While the church program is becoming more and more based on the power resources of the age—finance and bureaucracy—members in "secular" vocations likewise enter more and more deeply into the power structure of our civilization. While it is evident that much of our past nonconformity has been mere misguided cultural obscurantism, our "broadening" bears the marks of assimilation, of rising respectability, rather than true prophetic and redemptive witness.

I must ask your forbearance at these strong words. They are not spoken to condemn anyone. I fervently believe that in spite of the misconceptions in which we all partake, Christ receives us. There are many who hold perhaps most or all of the above misunderstandings, but who in accordance with their knowledge have given themselves to Christ, and He has received them. But that is a matter other than the question before us here.

What Do We Propose to Do?

Before any concrete suggestions can be made, it must be noted that no over-all answer is possible. To attempt such answer would simply reflect our mistakes in our present approach which assumes that we can save ethnic Mennonitism and receive a genuine revival as well.

Reorganization holds little promise. We would see hope in developments as the following.

1. In the willingness to grant a degree of the indigenous character of the church abroad, and in the acceptance of a decentralized I-W program are inklings of a higher way that seems to have broken for a brief moment through the clouds. The trend in places to grant greater congregational autonomy constitutes at least a negative gain in the sense of the removal of external limitations.

2. The removal of external restraining authority, however, can be helpful only if it is carried forward on an inner recovery of essence. In every congregation of the land, it is possible at any time to begin a constructive new approach, not through a new teaching program but through a new message, through a new breakthrough of the power of God.

3. It must become the goal of all who preach and teach to "present every man mature in Christ." Specifically this will require the kind of congregational life which will unite every member in an intimate, personal fellowship, where each is engaged in the destiny of the fellowship, a fellowship responsible in its own right under Christ for the life of every member.

4. We must be ready to allow the Spirit to create afresh, even when it means the bypassing or dismantling of our most cherished programs. Knowing how renewal has come in the past through "unofficial" initiative, it is too much to expect that the leadership as a whole can be won in stage one, and then the masses in stage two. Yet much could come if as leaders we could meet to await a fresh unction, which could call us into new commitment and new units of fellowship to go out in sacrificial witness. This proposal is "illogical," but it could well be that some of us—or all—would be called to disperse in bands of united, witnessing believers, abandoning the security and prestige of our position to hasten to proclaim the coming of our Lord. Is this not really what we proclaim? Is not this the meaning of the figure of the corn of wheat? It could be.

5. There is dire need for concerted effort and larger fellowship in the Kingdom. There is no doubt a legitimate place for some "agency" approaches. But these must be recognized for what they

are—structures of this age, ever standing under the demands of the living Christ in our midst. They in themselves are not the church visible but can be the means whereby Christians accomplish certain tasks. As E. A. Litton, an Anglican writer, has pointed out so aptly, "Every theory of the Church, whether it profess to be Romanist or not, which teaches that its true being lies in its visible characteristics, adopts instinctively the Romish notes and rejects the Protestant" (quoted by J. M. Kik in *Christianity Today*, May 27, 1957, p. 37).

6. Basically, we do not propose, however, that one can sketch in advance the route that the Spirit will take. An alternative "plan" to our present plan cannot be advanced, if by this is meant an alternative blueprint. We need not a new form developed from without, but a new flow of life from within. But we can appeal to this group to examine afresh the real import of the faith we confess, and to return to our respective places, determined to seek and to wait with our fellow Christians, that Christ and His Church may be formed anew within and among us.

What Are Our Concerns?

John Howard Yoder

I

There appears to be some sort of group mind and common concern growing in certain Mennonite circles, whose visible form is occasional in the publication of *Concern* and annual in study conferences; it makes itself heard outside the Mennonite Church mainly in matters having to do with nonresistance, and inside Mennonitism thus far mainly in matters having to do with church order. Its membership is undefinable, it is not an organized movement for which anyone can speak, yet it has sufficient body that people can ask what it's up to. This paper, written in April, 1955, and therefore not fully up to date, is an attempt, purely personal, to answer the question.

II

Sociologically, the group begins with people who shared in some degree the experiences of CPS, MCC, study of history and theology, travel abroad, evangelism and the peace witness. Not all are (Old) Mennonite but most have had contact with the revival of interest in Anabaptist studies, and many have been at Goshen. None of these factors suffice to explain their development, however, since many who underwent the same environmental influences did not come to the same conclusions.

III

There is a definite relation between the group's convictions and reactions, and the new understanding of the Anabaptist movement. The Anabaptist fad in American Mennonite circles is already a generation old, but this group has gone beyond studying the Anabaptists and admiring their depth of conviction, and reached the conclusion that on many points they were right and should be followed. The claim is not that the Anabaptist movement was infallible, but that on a surprising number of points they were led to right answers, which retain an exemplary value for our time. Since terms like "Christian, " "Biblical, " and "evangelical" are no longer sufficiently meaningful, and since some label or another is unavoidable, the group accepts the Anabaptist position, by and large, and from it directs its message toward both Mennonites and non-Mennonites. The group considers itself committed to the Mennonite fellowship in which its members grew up, insofar as that fellowship is willing to be renewed by rededication to its own heritage and to Biblical faith.

IV

The group's unity is more a set of common reaction patterns than a doctrine; any effort at doctrinal description will be artificial, more an attempt to group un-synthesized ideas than to demonstrate the unity of a ripe doctrinal system, which the group neither has nor desires. The choice of a classifying principle is purely subjective; some members would make the key word "pneumatic"; for others it would be "Biblicism." For simplicity's sake I shall speak here of the attributes of the church. For Roman Catholicism the church is defined by sacraments and hierarchy; for the churches of the Reformation by right preaching and sacraments, perhaps discipline; for liberalism by good intentions, for fundamentalism by true doctrine on certain selected questions; for spiritualism it is interior and undefinable. The Anabaptists had another answer, and we think they were right. To enumerate the marks of the church will thus permit describing the position which unites the members of the group and constitutes its message within and without Mennonitism.

V

The Church is the fellowship of those who have responded to the call of discipleship.

1. This involves no claim to perfection, and the interpretations of certain historians according to which the Anabaptists thought themselves to be perfect are incorrect, based on confusion between the theological definition of the church and its sociological realization. The question is not whether the Christian *is* perfect, but whether he should be.

2. "Discipleship" is the best word we have found to refer to the full intention of God with man. It denotes a synthesis of fellowship with God and obedience to His will, as revealed in Christ. This synthesis is to be distinguished from
    a. legalism and liberalism, which try to define the obedience without the fellowship;
    b. extreme Lutheranism, which is interested in achieving fellowship with God but not primarily in obedience;
    c. some kinds of orthodoxy which seek only correct doctrine about fellowship or obedience .

3. This means that concrete ethical teaching is possible, that valid knowledge about the good is available. The church is the agent through which ethical decisions are made, on the basis of Scripture and under the promised guidance of the Holy Spirit. This view of the basis of ethics is to be distinguished from
    a. Reformation Protestantism, in which ethical norms were derived from society ("ethics of vocation");
    b. most contemporary Protestantism, in which there are no ethical norms, each individual following his own conscience.

    An example may be the different understandings of the word "love." When the reformers read the love commandment, it meant to them, "you are free to do as you think best," and meant that they should aim at the establishment of a stable social order, making ethical choices on the pragmatic basis in a conservative tone of mind.

    When the Anabaptists read the same commandment, it meant, "you are bound to act the way love acted in Christ." Instead of ratifying the existing order the command transcended it, commanding suffering, not stability.

4. On this basis (and not on any other) discipline is possible within the fellowship: i.e., on the basis of the common conviction that the unity of the church is unity in discipleship. This discipline is not, however, based upon the automatic semi-mechanical application of rules against certain behavior (the error of some Mennonite legalism), but on an individual, local, Spirit-led process of growth together. If someone is finally excluded from the fellowship, it is not because he broke such and such a rule, but because he shows himself no longer desirous of living in the unity of the group's commitment to discipleship.

5. The whole view of discipleship assumes also that obedience is possible; not in the sense of a claim to have achieved purity, which would be looking man-ward, but in the sense of faith that God gives what He commands, so that man's imperfection has no place in the study of ethics. *Simul justus et peccator* is allowable as an historical observation; but it is illegitimate in the realm of faith and ethics.

VI

The unit of action and authority in the church is the local congregation.

1. This we affirm as over against
    a. confessionalism, which defines the church via a doctrinal statement,
    b. episcopal or presbyterian-synodical views, which define it mechanically,
    c. constantinian views, which define it geographically, provincially, nationally,
    d. pietism, cell movements, and other *ecclesiolae*, which have the congregation but distinguish between it and the church.

2. There is such a thing as the Church Universal, composed of all believers. It has no fixed sociological form, so that those who have eyes only for sociological structures call it "invisible." This Church Universal becomes visible already whenever two or three believers

meet under the sign of their common faith, thus also in an accidental conversation, in a denominational agency, or in an interchurch meeting. But it becomes really visible in terms of action and authority, when there is sufficient temporal continuity, geographical contiguity, and exchange of convictions and concerns for a unity to form whose core is a common commitment to discipleship.

3. A denomination (Mennonite branch, pan-Mennonite collaboration, or any other Roman or non-Roman super-congregational body) is neither a church nor the Church. It is justified as an instrument of fellowship, study, service or witness:

    a. when it does, in common, and with the consent of the churches:

        (1) a job which because of its size or because of the dangers of waste and overlapping should not be done on a smaller scale;

        (2) a job which should not be done on a larger scale because of lack of agreement or the dangers of bigness. (Note that the existence of the denomination on any level must therefore be defended both against the claims of larger groups and against those of the congregations.)

    b. when it does not take itself for the Church, limiting discussion and fellowship on the basis of denominational adherence. What disquiets us in certain Mennonite circles is not false theory about the Church so much as the assumption in practice that when we say "the Church" we mean our organization.

    c. when it is open to new needs, to structural changes, and even conceivably to its own extinction when its function can better be carried out on another higher or lower level.

VII

The authority in the church is the Bible.

1. No one would disagree with this statement; the differences come out in the use made of it. The Roman Church reads the Bible within the walls of her teaching authority, and expects no revela-

tion. The reformers really looked for revelation, i.e. for final authority, but only in terms of the questions they asked it. The same was true of Müntzer and the Münsterites. The Anabaptists differed in that they had sufficient detachment not only to ask the Bible their own questions, but also to ask the Bible what questions the Bible meant to answer. The other approaches led to orthodoxy, which means a stopping point attained; question put to Scripture, Scripture's answer to that question, a system built on that answer. The Anabaptists came quickly to definite positions, but by a more circular and less final study process; Scripture's answer to the first question is carried to the church, and thus serves to formulate a new question for which an answer must be sought, thus progressively purging out of the system one's unconscious presuppositions and getting more objectively at what the Bible itself is interested in. The issue in the sixteenth century was not whether the Bible was authority, but how its authority was to be lived. The Anabaptists were more successful in keeping Scriptural authority alive because

   a. they were willing to challenge the concept of "Christian society."
   b. they were willing to challenge traditional theological formulations.
   c. their interest in discipleship provided a new impetus to re-examination because in the search for discipleship new problems always arise, whereas if one stops with the concern for orthodoxy, one comes to the end of the problems.
   d. the brotherhood replaced the hierarchy and the theologians as the agent responsible for putting questions to Scripture.
   e. their attack on theology was (differently from that of the Spiritualizers) not on the discipline as such but on the legitimacy of certain sets of concepts and presuppositions.

2. In time, however, the Anabaptists boiled down this attitude to an orthodoxy of their own, so that today there exists no clear answer to the questions raised by the collision between Biblical authority and modern thought. The following answers are insufficient:
   a. The orthodoxies which still ask no questions.
   b. Fundamentalism is an inadequate term to cover a whole field. Taking it to designate the best thought of those who accept

the label, insofar as we know and understand them (and we should know them better), their answers seem to be insufficient in the following respects:
  (1) A Christian is defined first of all by his doctrinal beliefs.
  (2) A certain number of doctrinal points are "fundamental"; they are worth arguing about, others are not. This reflects a particular stage of the debate with modernism a half-century ago. That the debate with unbelief revolves around exactly the same points today would be hard to prove.
  (3) Some Fundamentalists go still further and say that someone who doesn't agree with their formulation of these twelve points does not believe the Gospel; that means that the points in question are themselves the Gospel. That also would be hard to prove Biblically, but it is the claim they make when they refuse the title "evangelical" to anyone but themselves.
  (4) Refusal to discuss, also a possible answer, means a hidden philosophy, unwilling to undergo examination.
c. Neo-Biblicism or Biblical realism, a school of thought just really beginning to take shape, owes its origin to several lines of development.
  (1) Rationalism forced what orthodoxy refused; its positivistic objective analysis asked the Bible what it really had to say. After a prolonged adolescence resulting from the parental domination of orthodoxy, the tradition of honest and technically capable scholarship is coming to maturity at a position nearer to Anabaptism than to either orthodoxy or liberalism.
  (2) For one thing, this objective scholarship has discovered that the Bible makes claims to authority; different perhaps from the claims made for it by Fundamentalism, but still far different from the meager devotional and literary value liberalism was willing to admit.
  (3) Those theologians with a systematic or philosophical interest have discovered that the Biblical view of man,

of values, of matter and spirit, etc., is more adequate to meet reality than is any purely philosophical set of ideas. This is a proof by experience, not by authority, but it has come out at the same place.

d. Liberalism in its classical form has nothing to offer on this question. "Neo-orthodoxy" is not a position but a continuum with an essentially liberal starting point, which in the face of certain issues approaches Biblical realism to a greater or lesser degree.
e. Our only conclusion for the moment is that there is as yet no satisfying doctrine of Biblical authority. It is probably to be sought in starting not with a philosophy about what revelation is but with exegesis about what revelation wants to do. We should keep close both to intelligent Fundamentalism and to neo-Biblicism, since the answer lies somewhere between the two.
f. The first question for us, and it is a question which we may work on without having a finished answer to the other, is what the Bible says, not a doctrine of authority. In general it will become evident that we attribute to the Bible more concrete authority over us, in the fields of sociology, ethics, church order, atonement, and economics, than do those who are ready to fight at the drop of a hat for a doctrine of Biblical authority or inspiration.

VIII

The Church is a Separation. One of the great theological originalities of the Anabaptists was that only they, of all the branches of the Reformation, gave any theological meaning to the concept "world." The Constantinian churches could not speak meaningfully of the "world" since they had baptized it into the church. When in Matthew 13 Jesus explains the parable of the tares in the wheat by saying, "the field is the world," the reformers insisted that that meant the Church.

The Anabaptists applied this discovery to their ways of thinking about the church, about ethics, even about atonement. It is the insight behind their specific stands on

a. nonresistance, nonswearing, nontribunals, non-participation in government; all of this a refusal to deal with evil the way the world does.
b. eschatology; a refusal to agree with the world on the meaning of history. The reformers also had a strong feeling about the near end of the world, but for none of them did this have the definite relation to present tensions between church and world which it did in the New Testament and in Anabaptism.
c. voluntary church membership.
d. missions; by definition a *Landeskirche* (territorial church) cannot do mission work.
e. nonconformism in other fields of ethics; luxury and avarice, artificial politeness, alcoholism, ambition.
f. the state; if they had had time they would have worked out, in line with their church-world understanding, the lines of prophetic witness to the state; telling the statesman that if he refuses to accept the Gospel, he should at least be an honest statesman.

IX

The church is missionary and led by the Spirit. These two necessities are well enough admitted to need little further development, although they are not a part of orthodox Lutheran, Reformed, or Anglican doctrines of the true church. The main contribution of the Anabaptist position, however, is not to make these points, since they are already undisputable, but to demonstrate that they cannot be taken seriously without drawing certain other conclusions, such as separation from the world and congregationalism.

X

The Church is bigger than our own back yard. [For a more recent treatment of this question, cf. the author's series, "The Ecumenical Movement and the Faithful Church," in the *Gospel Herald* (Scottdale, Pennsylvania, Volume L (1957), numbers 3 (Jan 15) to 8 (Feb 19).]

1. The ways in which Christians and churches should have fraternal relations with one another are numerous:
   a. common work in service and witness
   b. common worship
   c. acquaintance with one another's concerns and needs
   d. reciprocal admonition where one or the other (or both) is wrong
   e. organizational union or federation in limited cases

   Only under the first of these heads is there any reason for stopping at the denominational level, and then even it depends on the specific job at hand; in all other respects mentioned, unity is a positive Christian duty, except for the last.

2. This is not our major point, but it is a fact that only the free church can consistently be "ecumenical" in the good sense of the word.
   a. Territorial or confessional churches cannot by definition be ecumenical; the most they can do is to recognize one another as being *also* valid churches.
   b. Episcopal and Orthodox churches are even less capable of being fraternally open; since the historical continuity which they alone possess is their definition of the church, the only way to have unity is to join them. This is real sectarianism.

3. The true vigor of ecumenical Christianity has in the past been in the free churches. Their congregational base permitted them to recognize any gathering of believers as a church; their mission emphasis and their refusal of national loyalties made them truly ecumenical years before the movement which bears the name. Especially noteworthy are
   a. the Brethren of the sixteenth century (i.e. the Biblical Anabaptists);
   b. the Friends of the seventeenth;
   c. the Brüdergemeinde and the Brethren Church from the eighteenth; (as well as pietism and Methodism to a lesser degree); and
   d. the ("Plymouth") Brethren of the nineteenth (George Müller).

4. It may also be demonstrated that the vigor of the present "ecumenical" movement is due to forces which, though not working in

the form of institutional churches, had some of the characteristics of free-church movements. One may point to

a. the line Moody—Mott—Student Volunteer Movement—International Missionary Council—Student Christian Movement—World Council of Churches;

b. the line "Association for International Friendship Through the Churches," which produced as a branch the IFOR [International Fellowship of Reconciliation —Ed.] as well as contribution to the foundation of the World Council of Churches; in Germany between the wars, the ecumenical movement and the Christian peace movement were the same man;

c. the Confessing Church in Germany.

Not that we approve in every way of everything done by these groups; in many ways they bear the marks of the age of liberalism; further, they are pietist rather than free-church in the sense that they consent to be an *ecclesiola* which does not challenge the institutional structure of the worldly church. Yet they all bear, to a greater or lesser degree, the marks of the free church; they are international, missionary, ethical, eschatological, able to see the church as an event.

5. The existing agencies of international or interdenominational fellowship all have certain "hobbies" which make it undesirable for the time being for us to make a total commitment to any of them; all are in some way or other "Constantinian."

a. The National Council of Churches in the States is particularly interested in bringing about organizational merger. This is barking up a wrong tree. Organizational merger is not one of the marks of the Church of Christ; organizational collaboration is justified only when its goals are defined and the organization presents the best adapted way to reach those goals and no others. The NCC further has a slant in social ethics which, although improving in some ways, cannot be called clearly prophetic at the most critical points. It gives a blanket approval to militarism, in practice though not in theory, which makes it impossible for a peace church to be enthusiastic about membership.

b. The National Association of Evangelicals and its offspring, the World Evangelical Fellowship, are at many points closer to us in external and doctrinal respects, and some Mennonite groups are officially affiliated with the NAE or its branches. It also, however, has several hobbies which make it impossible for us to seek full membership:
   (1) a form of antiliberalism which no longer speaks to the present debate with much more subtle forms of unbelief.
   (2) a degree of pro-Americanism, republicanism, militarism, and antisocialism which is not compatible with separation from the world.
   (3) a refusal to discuss matters on which members do not agree (form or age of baptism, church order), thus maintaining the appearance of a greater degree of unity than really exists, as well as making a distinction which is questionable between essentials and nonessentials.

We should thus maintain relationships with all these agencies on a personal or observer basis, but for the time being membership does not seem to be indicated, unless clearly limited to conversation.

6. There are a number of arguments commonly brought against interchurch relationships, most of them wrong, and most of them based on failure to understand the relation of discipline to the local congregation.
   a. A recent letter in the official NAE publication said that the NAE's reason for existence is the command to be separate from unbelievers. That command, however, was given to a congregation, and its specific reference was probably to marriage. In no case is it an argument against relationships with other congregations, even if they are imperfect or even wrong on some points.
   b. The separatist tradition, appealing in our circles to the examples of Zurich in 1525 or the Mennonite Brethren beginnings in 1860, thinks that withdrawal is a way to be faithful. But the true church is formed by withdrawal from the world, not from other churches. Neither the Anabaptists or the MB's

took the initiative in withdrawing; they were kicked out, something radically different. When there is unfaithfulness in a church, the unfaithful should leave, not the faithful. The faithful should complain, appealing to Scripture and asking for discipline; only when the entire body refuses to listen and takes the initiative in breaking fellowship is a break to be accepted.

c. Thus the fact that in a given interchurch situation other churches are unfaithful is no reason for not conversing with them; that reason exists only if they refuse to listen. At the time of the division of Princeton Seminary, there was mutual refusal to listen; likewise at the time of the birth of Anabaptism, and when the Mennonites withdrew from the Federal Council of Churches; such is not the case now. If our witness again is refused, we will again be justified in withdrawing; at present, however, we are not so justified.

Organization and Church

John W. Miller

During the past several decades, Western civilization has experienced what has been called an "organizational revolution." The Quaker economist Kenneth E. Boulding recently described this revolution as one of the most remarkable features of our American society (*The Organizational Revolution*, 1953).

Just a century ago in America there were no farm organizations of any importance, no American Legion, practically no labor organization; in Washington, no Department of Agriculture, no Department of Labor; and, other than the Masons, virtually no fraternal organizations. Today according to a 1949 census published by the U.S. Department of Commerce, there are over four thousand "voluntary organizations" in the United States—a figure which does not include business enterprises or organs of government. Boulding notes in the opening pages of his discussion that this development has crept upon us silently, and that consequently "we are still often a hundred years behind the times—still thinking in terms of a society in which organizations are rather small and weak, and in which the family is the dominant institution."

It was in the midst of this revolution that the American Mennonites began to step out of their generations-long role as "die Stillen im Lande" ("the quiet in the land"), and along with many other Protestant denominations sought to play a more responsible part in today's world. It was natural that new spiritual impulses should express themselves in new forms and natural, too, that some of these forms should be adopted *en bloc* from the contemporary culture. In a world that was rapidly learning the techniques and forms of organizational procedure, an awakened church began therefore to employ these same procedures for her own ends. Mission boards were organized, schools established, relief committees set up, publishing enterprises founded and much more. So it came about that the churches incorporated within their bosoms a vast network of organizational enterprises. It is this vigorous organizational activity which many are now pointing to as the most obvious sign of the health and vitality of the American Church.

The fact that this organizational activity within the Church reflects in large part the ways of the age should, however, give some pause. It is at least apparent that organizational activities in themselves do not belong to that which is unique to the Christian faith and life. The fact that Mennonites and other Christian groups have mastered the techniques, for example, of running schools, using radio, and publishing books is in itself no sign of special Christian merit. In all this we have simply incorporated into our own life the ways and forms of our technological civilization. This is not to deny that the motive and purpose of these organizational activities is Christian, but only to question an unquestioning optimism respecting these activities as such and to lay the groundwork for the central concern of this essay, namely, what is the relation of these organizational activities to the Church?

I

It is hard to escape the impression that there is a widespread feeling among members of the Church that these organizational activities are the Church. It is true that sometimes an attempt is made to distinguish between this network of institutional operations and the Church proper by speaking of them as "arms" of the Church or "the Church at work," but rarely is the distinction sharply or consistently maintained. To give money to the work of the Church has come to mean by and large to give it to Church institutions. In the same way full-time Church work has come to mean, for many, full-time work in one of our Church institutions.

The confusion involved in such attitudes becomes apparent only as we remember precisely what the Church is. For the purposes of this brief article, we may refer to the familiar but crucial words of Christ in

Matt. 18:20. There Jesus lays down in one sentence what many have felt to be the simplest and most basic definition of the Church: "Where two or three are gathered together in my name, there am I in the midst of them." This definition has three parts, and each is vital to a true understanding of the Church.

First, it defines the Church as a gathering of at least two or three. The Church is not represented by an individual but by people who have stepped out of their isolation into a "togetherness far deeper than any mere camaraderie"(Cranfield).

Second, the Church gathering takes place in the "name" of Christ. This involves more than a gathering for worship in the typical Protestant sense. Throughout the Bible, the "name" is more than a tag. It signifies the person and all that he is and stands for. To gather in the name of Jesus then is to gather in conscious remembrance of His person and cause. Practically speaking, this involves actively remembering and retelling the words and deeds of Jesus. Julius Schniewind rightly suggests that Matthew 18:20 could stand as a title to the New Testament Gospels, "for the deeds and words of Jesus were only reported because it was known that the exalted Christ Himself was present in the fellowship, there where His words and deeds, His life and death were remembered."

But to gather in the "name" of Jesus certainly involves more than just remembering and retelling; it involves obedience as well (Matt. 7:24 ff.). Insofar as the words and deeds of Jesus call us into new paths of attitude and conduct, they must be heeded as well as heard. When we gather in the "name" of Jesus we remember Him in order to obey Him and to give ourselves to the same cause for which He stood. Without going into detail here about what that cause is (See section III below), it can be said that it is something whole and indivisible as far as human relations are concerned. Jesus Himself summed it up as that restoration of the whole man in a loving relation to God and his fellow men, which is the fulfillment of law and prophets. It is that true fellowship of totally committed disciples to which Jesus called His followers already during His earthly ministry and which Paul loved to refer to as the body of Christ when it appeared in response to the summons of the good news at place after place all over the Roman Empire.

To such a gathering, thirdly, the living Christ comes through His Spirit. "There am I in the midst of them," Jesus promises. By this the community of men and women, met and bound together for the cause of Christ, becomes the spiritual body of Christ representing on earth the purposes of the heavenly Lord. Bearing Christ's name and indwelt by Christ's presence, the Church is nothing less than the reincarnation of His ascended person.

If we measure the character of our organizational gatherings by this simple but far-reaching definition of a church gathering, there seems to exist a marked difference between the two especially at the point of the second of the three characteristics mentioned above. In the various organizational activities of the churches, men and women come together to do good works, but can we say that they gather in the "name" of Christ, if we think of the "name" as standing for the whole cause of Christ in calling out a people who will live in the harmony of love and peace with God and their fellow men? In our church schools, for example, Christian men and women come together for the education of youth. But the education of youth, while in itself a worthy enterprise, could hardly be interpreted as coextensive with the complete cause of Christ. The faculties of our schools do not make up the Christian community into which we invite the lost, nor do they intend to. They are not congregational gatherings in the "name" of Christ, nor do they intend to be. In this respect the objectives of those who organize themselves for the work of education are self-limited. The same type of self-limitation is characteristic of every one of our denominational institutions. In fact it is the very genius of the organizational approach that it isolates a part in order to work more efficiently at it. In this sense and for this reason these segmented organizational gatherings fall short of being "churches."

The distinction referred to here between gatherings in the "name" of Christ and organizational gatherings is one that is at least unconsciously recognized among us especially in the practice of introducing new members into the Church. So far as I know, no Christian group baptizes members in the setting of Church organizations but always in the congregational setting. Apparently this is done because it is still felt that congregational gatherings represent the Christian cause in a way that organizational gatherings do not. This distinction, which we continue to recognize in an unconscious way, must be rigorously and consciously maintained in both thought and terminology. Otherwise the profound priority and importance of the congregational gatherings over against the organizational gatherings will be lost, and the true cause of Christ will be horribly confused before a needy world.

II

The question remains yet whether or not the organizational revolution which has taken place both in the world and in the Church during the past decades only gives rise to a different type of gathering from a true Church-congregational gathering or in addition sets in motion forces which, potentially, at least, could act destructively on the life of God's people. Many who have thought deeply about the effects of this revolution on society as a whole have declared that its influence on the life of man in general has been far from uniformly good. While the technological age has brought untold material abundance to man and demonstrated its worth in a physical sense, it may well turn out that this has been achieved at the price of tremendous spiritual loss.

Perhaps the deadliest effect of the organizational revolution, and the one most often mentioned by secular and religious analysts alike, is the almost inevitable process of dehumanization. The French Catholic philosopher Gabriel Marcel commented incisively on the point at issue here (in an essay on "The Limitations of Industrial Civilization") when he spoke of "agglomerations replacing cities" and of these agglomerations as being the very "embodiment of uprootedness."

In this same connection he writes:

> In such a world the mass transfers of populations which have taken place in the totalitarian countries should no longer be considered an anomaly. On the contrary, they may well become the rule once the vital link is broken between man and his environment and people are seen as mere units of production—as machines which are needed here or there for reasons connected with the general economy and whose feelings are of not the slightest interest. Indeed, perhaps it would be best so to train these men-machines that their needs and feelings would become atrophied and in the end vanish!

It is such observations as these which compel Marcel and many others to wonder whether the liberation of man from the forces of nature brought about by the technological revolution might not in the end turn into a slavery.

What has happened to society in general in the wake of the organizational revolution can just as easily happen in the Church. Even when baptized by the Church for its own purposes, the organizational approach spawns attitudes and breeds patterns that cannot help but threaten the binding and wholeness of the congregational gathering—that one gathering where wholeness and humanity in the truest sense must at all cost be preserved if the world is to have salt and light. The segmentation of life and the consequent "dehumanizing" of personal relationships which follow so inevitably in the wake of the organizational revolution is not overcome by attaching the organizational approach to an abstracted Christian cause. Nor can we add together all the piecemeal organizational efforts of the Church to carry out the purposes of Christ and suppose that they together sum up the "name" or the whole purpose for which Christ stands. For the work which Christ came to do is just that which the organizational approach by necessity must in part undo. Christ called men, as we have suggested, into a whole gathering of wholly dedicated people. The effects of the organizational revolution are therefore perhaps nowhere more dangerous than here where they threaten to lead to the disintegration of the all-encompassing life of God's kingdom and God's people. At this point the organizational approach may destroy what it hopes to serve and for all its well-meaning turn light into darkness.

III

Perhaps the Old Testament itself gives us the best historical example of such a thing actually happening. Under Solomon and his successors, a kind of organizational revolution entered into the life of the Old Testament people of God. The magnificent cultural achievements of the Solomonic era were carried out only by means of a vast restructuring of the primitive tribal and familial units. During these years, life focused more and more in the great metropolitan centers where the rich and the powerful headquartered. Life in the village communities was rent and torn and the old locus of decision-making, the village gate, became a powerless, irrelevant institution.

It was in this setting that the great prophetic tradition of the Old Testament arose to call men back to the old ways, the original intention of God for His people. The fundamental note of this tradition was sounded by the first of this prophetic line, Amos, who in his clearest positive statement calls the men of his time to work for the reinvigoration of justice in the gate. Only those who gather in the true way of the old times, when men morning by morning ordered their lives according to the living word of justice spoken by God without fail (Zephaniah 3:5) could expect to survive the catastrophic judgment which God must pour out on all sinful mankind (Amos 5:15).

The prophetic witness to the value of the gathering at the gate is only an Old Testament counterpart to Christ's own teaching concerning the importance of the gathering of the two or three in His "name, " and cannot be understood as a kind of nostalgic primitivism, unless we are ready to pass the same verdict on Christ's teaching. Both the teachings of Christ and the prophets are rooted rather in a deep awareness that the fundamental sin of man is his puffed up, acquisitive heart, and the only answer to man's predicament is a new order, which must begin at the level of the whole man in his relation to God and his fellow men. Micah's famous formulation of the ancient requirements of God (6:8), for example, cuts through all the superficialities of human relationships to expose a social order for which no piecemeal organizational procedures could ever be adequate.

Thus to "do justice," as the Biblical tradition understands it, is the work, *not* of an organization, but of a people who in the active decisions of day-by-day life seek to uphold a basic respect for the freedom and well-being of each other. To "love kindness" is again, not a quality that can be represented by a committee or a program, but is rather the activity of men with each other, for whom covenant loyalty and steadfast love are the highest goals of existence. Likewise to "walk humbly with God" is the work of those who know that the resources for man's ultimate salvation lie outside of human calculation and become available, in fact, just at that point where human programs cease.

The Old and New Testaments summarize the point at issue here when they speak of the chosen ones of God as a people rather than a nation: ". . . lo, a people dwelling alone, and not reckoning itself among the nations!" prophesies Balaam, according to Numbers 23:9 (RSV). Throughout the Old Testament, Israel is consistently spoken of as the people (*'am*) of Jahweh, never as Jahweh's nation (*goi*). Martin Buber caught the profound significance of this distinction when he wrote that the God of the Bible wants to rule a people not a crowd. It is just this distinction between the crowdlike, swarming status of the nations, even with all their organizational genius and kingly control, and the divinely illuminated and ordered community of Israel on which poet, lawgiver and prophet in the Old Testament love to dwell. When the Apostle Peter writes then to the dispersed and suffering congregations of the early Church: "Once you were no people but now you are God's people" (I Peter 2:10, RSV), his words are charged with meaning.

IV

While then the study of the Bible and of history raises severe forebodings about the implications of the organizational revolution for the life of the Church, the conclusion of the whole matter is not necessarily that the one automatically excludes the other. The title of this article may still stand, "Organization *and* Church," and nothing that has been written above should be construed to mean "Organization vs. Church."

The weight of technological and organizational revolution which has come upon us cannot be abandoned, nor should it be. That would be an empty dream that supposed that spiritual renewal could lie at the end of a vast dismantling of our institutional machinery. The right procedure lies rather in an awakened awareness of the absolutely central importance of the congregational gatherings and their decisive place in the economy of God—a place that organization can never replace but only at best and in a limited sense serve. The point must never be lost that the decision to stake one's lot with the people of God in the assembly of the "two and three" is still the most important thing that anyone can do. Here is the place where the real cause of Christ is represented and the work of God done. Here is the place where the concept of "full-time commitment to the work of the Church" should find its truest expression. Where this sense of the importance of the congregational gathering becomes alive the various organizational programs of the Church will probably of themselves assume their true significance.

Property
A Problem in Christian Ethics

Herbert Klassen

Property has been a problem ever since man fell and was expelled from the Garden of Eden. Destined to eke out his existence in the struggle with nature, the primary necessities of life have provided man with an opportunity to express his selfishness and greed. There have always been evidences, it seems, of man's craving for things, bringing with it the resultant problems of exploitation, inequality, and poverty. But never before in the history of mankind, as in the last one hundred years, has the desire for material things been so exalted and so rewarding; and nowhere in the world are the problems caused by the possession of *much* property as real and as relevant as in North America.

It is sad to witness that the tremendous increases in capital and wealth in the Western world, and the all-pervading changes in the way of life and system of values that have accompanied these changes, have not aroused much serious concern in the Church. Most Protestant treatments of ethics have basically little to say on the problems of property and economics. Individualism and wealth have become so much a part of the Church of North America that there is little conscience concerning the complacency it has caused in its own ranks, or regarding the fact that sixty percent of the world's population goes to bed hungry every night.

The task of this paper is not to explore or criticize the morality of the modern economic order, but rather to seek to find what the Biblical teaching concerning property is, and how the Church has interpreted this teaching. The relevancy of these principles for the Church today is implied throughout the paper rather than stated, because of their nature and because of limitations of space.

The Christian approach to the problem of property cannot be explored in a vacuum: when Christ said, "Lay not up . . . treasures on earth," He turned to the positive side of God's intention and said, "but seek ye first the kingdom of God" (Matthew 6:19, 33). The one would in all likelihood have consequences for the other. When Paul said that covetousness is the source of all evil (Colossians 3:5; I Timothy 6:9–10) he based his indifference to property on the urgency of his eschatological hope. The problem of acquiring and using property thus cannot be divorced from the Biblical emphasis on the corporate character of the kingdom of God, and "community eschatology." If the intention of seeking first the kingdom of God is absent, no amount of casuistic regulation regarding the accumulation and use of property would be of any avail.

The Old Testament prophets expressed this very well in their criticism of Jewish economic accommodation. When debt slavery increased and Israel reverted back to an individualistic, competitive economy based on the practices of heathen nations, the pre-exilic prophets attacked not by condemning business life as such, but by giving a renewed call to loyalty.[2] Obedience to God's intention must always be the starting point. Any type of legalism that gives formal justification to compromise or that spells out sociologically the intention of God will always be attacked.

Within our complex economic structure, it would be futile to attempt a casuistic evaluation of what a "treasure on earth" is. Whether an automobile, a house, a farm, or a business is a "treasure" cannot be known until one has sought first the kingdom of God, and until eschatological hope and justice within the brotherhood have become a living reality. Where this is not the case, however, we must face the fact that the very urgent and practical warnings of Christ regarding property and wealth become mere empty phrases and pious repetitions.

The problem of the use and abuse of property is brought into sharper focus by the fact that neither the repeated warnings of God

2. G. Ernest Wright, *The Biblical Doctrine of Man in Society*, London: SCM Press Ltd., 1954, p. 145.

in the Old Testament concerning property nor those of Christ in the Gospels presuppose an absolute renunciation of property. Since it is not a matter of total renunciation of property or of unqualified acceptance of wealth, we must seek through the Holy Spirit a form that is an expression of God's intention for His people: to wit, a love community, a sharing brotherhood, the new Kingdom.

In developing our concept of property, it seems that two propositions have become apparent: first, that if you have a treasure on earth, your heart will be there, and you will be covetous; and second, that for a Christian, personal possession and use of property should be subordinated to sharing, to Church-brotherhood purpose and responsibility. Yet, even if these are granted as principles, it is evident that they afford no simple or final solution. It is the burden of this paper, however, that they do provide a necessary setting for a "better way," and that they do clarify some of the issues that the Church of every generation must face.

The Old Testament

It is generally agreed that the first Old Testament principle regarding property is that all property belongs to God, who is its Creator; and second, that being a gift of God, it is essentially good. The emphasis of Old Testament and New Testament alike, however, is on the moral dangers of property. Already in Deuteronomy 8 God warns the people:

> Take heed . . . lest, when you have eaten and are full, and have built goodly houses and live in them, and when your herds and flocks multiply, and your silver and gold is multiplied, and all that you have is multiplied, then your heart be lifted up, and you forget the Lord your God . . . and . . . you say in your heart, 'My power and the might of my hand have gotten me this wealth.'

In Psalm 49 David speaks of those who trust in their wealth, and boast themselves in the multitude of their riches: none of them can by any means redeem himself, that he should not see the pit. Isaiah also has a warning for the covetous: "Woe unto them that join house to house, that lay field to field" (Isaiah 5:8). This is an oft-repeated theme in the Old Testament. Wright has pointed out that material abundance was seen as evil in two situations: "when it led members of the community to a denial of their dependence upon and obedience to their Lord; and when it was gained at the expense and impoverishment of the weaker neighbor."[3]

It was the great mission of the prophets to uphold God's concern for social righteousness. They maligned those who destroy the restrictions of God's order and open the way to lust for power and possessions on the pattern of the great empires. They also attack the war profiteers, upstarts and moneymakers, who make profitable business out of the misery of the masses. The tricks of the corn usurers and land speculators are repeatedly exposed by the prophets. They bring to light a great temptation which springs from the development of the capitalistic economy and has a subtle appeal; the temptation to increase the number of economic goods and use them for the purpose of making more profit—as if that were an end in itself. They also attack another form of idolatry of material values—namely, the unprecedented growth of a life of pleasure. The fact that the love of pleasure and luxury becomes an idol, to which men would rather offer their sacrifices than to the God of the poor and the unprivileged, is the essential point of the prophets' scathing judgment on the civilization of their own day. In the eyes of the prophets, "every solemn acknowledgment of the God of their fathers, who had brought them out of slavery in Egypt, becomes a lie unless it leads on to the struggle for justice in human society."[4]

Because the Old Testament teaches that all property belongs to God, that it is a gift of God, and that it is consequently good does not mean that it encourages the possession of large private fortunes. Quite the contrary, for the Old Testament teaches that wealth among the people of God belongs not to an individual but to a whole family, clan or community. The individual holds his share only as organ and instrument of the fellowship of God's people. The law of the sabbatical year states: "At the end of every seven years thou shalt make a release. And this is the manner of the release: Every creditor that lendeth ought unto his' neighbor shall release it" (Deuteronomy 15:1ff). The law of the jubilee or liberty year, in which "ye shall return every man unto his possession" (Leviticus 25:13), is another indication of the emphasis in

---

3. Ibid., p. 144.

4. Walter Eichrodt, "The Question of Property in the Light of the Old Testament," *Biblical Authority for Today*, (ed. by Alan Richardson and W. Schweitzer), Philadelphia: Westminster Press, 1951, p. 270.

Old Testament law on community rights. These practices were contrary to the heathen nations round about them and were consequently strange to the Jews, even as practices contrary to the world would be offensive to the Church in our day.

Ordinary interest and usury are forbidden in the Old Testament because they involve making a profit out of a brother's misfortune. Lending was a duty to those in need, not a means of financial gain. "God tolerates no selfish accumulation of wealth, but demands instead obedience to *mishpat*, conformity to the good custom or justice. This morality is over and above strict justice, a virtue which is to roll down as an ever-flowing stream."[5] The early Israelite emphasis was upon property as a blessing, when social justice held it to an even distribution; the later maladministration of property and individualism caused the emphasis to fall on its moral dangers. From Eichrodt we learn that:

> . . . the land is not a thing which can be sold at will. Being the basis of the existence of the people, it belongs not to the individual, but to the community. Hence when Canaan was conquered it was divided among the tribes who again divided it among the different clans and families. But the clans have a permanent prior claim on the property, taking precedence on the individual's claim. . . . Since the clans can always redeem the land sold by the individual they preserve the basis of their existence unimpaired. For the land is the most important means of production; and the Old Testament legal system is concerned with ensuring that every citizen has access to this means of production by protecting the land from private speculation and administering it as communal property.[6]

We are not expected in the twentieth century to take over Old Testament agrarian laws in their historical form and apply them to our time. The point that we must recognize is the intent of those laws: that everyone should enjoy the profits of his own labor and not be cut off from free access to the means of production. Ownership of the means of production, if it cannot be transferred entirely to the community, must be removed from the risk of selfish misappropriation and placed at the service of all. No legal regulation should make it possible for goods which

---

5. C. L. Taylor, "Old Testament Foundations," *Christianity and Property*, (ed. by J. F. Fletcher), Philadelphia: Westminster Press, 1947, p. 24.

6. Eichrodt, op. cit., pp. 264–65.

are required for general use to be held back from the economic process and kept in reserve, in order to obtain a higher profit. As a member of the people of God, it is necessary to subordinate the use and possession of property to kingdom-of-God-purpose and responsibility. As an expression of God's will in the Old Testament, the message concerning property seems clear.

The New Testament

"Beware of all covetousness" is a warning that is often repeated in the New Testament. When Christ was asked to divide an inheritance, He refused, but He used the occasion to say: "Take heed, and beware of all covetousness; for a man's life does not consist in the abundance of his possessions" (Luke 12:15, RSV). Property is not inherently evil, but because the will of man is perverted, for him to possess material things for his own selfish purpose is positively sinful. The scribes and Pharisees, those who would not surrender their wills to Jesus, were attacked for devouring widows' houses and practicing extortion.

Jesus wants to place men in a position of complete poverty of spirit before God, and it is this that riches prevent (Matthew 5:3). Men come to trust in them and not in God, so that when death arrives suddenly, it makes their foolishness and final poverty evident (Luke 12:20–21). Men are deceived and confused by riches; they come to think that a man's life consists in the abundance of his possessions, not realizing that moths and rust consume these things (Matthew 6:19ff.). They hear the Word of God but the cares of the world and the deceitfulness of riches enter in and choke the Word, and it becomes unfruitful (Luke 8:14 ff.). Riches also lead men to make excuses, so that men will actually let a field or a few oxen stand in the way of obedience to the living Christ (Luke 14:18ff.). The rich young ruler sadly turned away when Christ laid His finger on his property (Matthew 19:21ff.). The greatest peril of wealth as stressed by Christ is that it leads to a hardness of heart which takes the form of indifference to the needs of others. The scribes and Pharisees and the story concerning Dives and Lazarus (Luke 16:19–31) are convincing examples of this truth.

The New Testament teaching regarding property is very directly related to the breaking in of the kingdom of God and the imminent end of the age. Christ Himself, while preaching the kingdom of God, held no property; He was content to let Himself be provided for by the substance of a few women. When He sent out His disciples, He charged them that they should take nothing for their journey, save a staff only; no bread, no wallet, no money in their purse (Luke 9:3ff.). It is only within the context of the Kingdom that this indifference to possessions can be understood. Although Christ's call to poverty, as in the instance of the rich young ruler, might not necessarily be thought of as a general call, it does seem that within the Kingdom, one holds things at the direction of the brotherhood and for the extension of the Kingdom. The danger of private possessions is that they divert men from the singleness of heart that the Kingdom demands. No division of the heart is possible: one cannot serve God and mammon (Matthew 6:24). If a man has wealth, his heart is there, and it is because of this that it is very difficult to enter the Kingdom. Christ reminds us that this is no cause for despair, for God can help a man become willing to leave his possessions behind and so enter the Kingdom (Matthew 19:23, 24).

Jesus's ideal is not a flight into the alone, for the total commitment of the disciple finds its embodiment in the corporate character of the Kingdom. Sacrificial love and service are inevitable parts of the new life, and from these springs the necessity of sharing one's possessions. When Peter said that they had left all to follow Him, Jesus said:

> Truly, I say to you, there is no one who has left house or brothers or sisters or mother or father or children or lands, for my sake and for the gospel, who will not receive a hundredfold now in this time, houses and brothers and sisters and mothers and children and lands, with persecutions, and in the age to come eternal life. (Mark 10:29–30, RSV)

This can be understood best in the context of the new society, the sharing brotherhood, where one's own life and possessions are shared with the brethren. He who does not hold all things in trust as a faithful steward waiting for the Kingdom, and he who does not give, share, and relieve the needy, is excluded from the Kingdom (Matthew 25:31–46). Along with all these warnings there is a mood of urgency evident in the Gospels which makes one feel that the whole business of holding possessions is part of an order of things that will soon come to an end.

After Pentecost the same emphases are present, with one difference: a dynamic community has been formed which now seeks to put love into effect. Wright has the following to say about the early Church described in Acts:

> The so-called "communism" of the early community in Jerusalem has often been misinterpreted. It was not a complete programme for the life of all Christians, but actually a means to alleviate poverty. The Gospel appealed at first to few rich people, and there were many poor in the economically parasitic city of Jerusalem. The common life of the disciples with Jesus had instilled in them a generous spirit, and this type of life was now extended as a means of caring for the poor. (Acts 4:32-38)[7]

It would be quite wrong to say that what Christ said to the rich young ruler applied automatically to *all* Christians, and in the same manner it would be wrong to say that *every* Christian group should slavishly copy the early Church pattern. But it would be equally wrong to say that Christ and the Holy Spirit were mistaken, and that what they said applied only to the *one* rich ruler and the *Jerusalem* Church. If in any age and culture material abundance is once more leading members of the community to a denial of their dependence upon and obedience to their Lord and is causing injustice within the group, the eternal Words of Christ might become once more a call to poverty or sharing. If at some point in history a local church is no longer of one heart and soul, if there is little devotion to the apostles' teaching, to the breaking of bread and prayers, if members rarely partake of food with glad and generous hearts, if testimony to the resurrection of the Lord Jesus is relatively powerless, and if the Lord is no longer adding day by day those who are being saved, then one might have cause to ask whether the private possession of earthly treasures is not one of the reasons for hindering "fellowship."

It is impossible to discuss the early Church and property without facing the problem of social structure. It seems obvious that divine *agape* does not express itself necessarily in *one* specific form. That it must, however, express itself in *some* type of structure is clear. Some of the directives and principles underlying the work of the Holy Spirit in creating the first form that the Church took are to be found in the New

---

7. Wright, *op. cit.*, pp. 146,147.

Testament. Some of the characteristics of the Church as the Body of Christ help to bring the question of structure into focus.

The new, abiding unity between the members in the Body *must* have some social consequences. Where many individuals share an experience so intimate as the "partnership of the Son of God," there must be a very close unity among them. If they are moved and governed by the same Spirit they are one at the deepest levels of life. "When a number of individuals with varying and even clashing interests have been caught by a revolutionary force which has made some one new interest mean more to each than any of his previous interests, then a new unity is inevitably created. This is actually what happened to the early Christians."[8]

This new unity in Christ rests on a most intensely individual experience, and yet each member of the Body finds real significance only from his place in the whole. Jesus knew, however, that the individual can only enter the Kingdom by denying all self-seeking individualism, and that consequently it would not attract men of wealth and position from conventional society. This did not lead Christ to express any desire to modify the present social order. He placed the eternal social order sharply over against the present temporal society and desired that it remain in this tension until He returns. He had no intention of rectifying the present situation in terms of social reform such as the modern world usually advocates. And yet Petry says: "Not thinking primarily of contemporary social change, he insures it by demanding a precedence of devotion to the eternal society and its standards. . . . It is evident that such an eschatological consecration by the lowly in heart gives to them, now, a kingdom character of communal life and mutuality that cannot escape having social consequences."[9]

This introduces eschatology and its bearing on the structure of the early Church. The otherworldliness which characterized the whole thought of the early period is a combination of a sense of the world's evil and the expectation of its early break-up at the *parousia* of Jesus. "From this point of view, property appears not only as an essentially ephemeral and perishable thing, but as a hindrance and an entanglement."[10] Petry

8. C. Harold Dodd, *The Meaning of Paul for Today*, London: Swarthmore Press, 1920, p. 139.

9. Ray C. Petry, *Christian Eschatology and Social Thought*, New York: Abingdon Press, 1956, p. 68.

10. C. J. Cadoux, *The Early Church and the World*, Edinburgh: T & T Clark, 1925, p. 127.

says that "Christian eschatology has been denominated as community eschatology. It never deals with individuals as if isolated from groups; nor can it think of any ultimate grouping that does not give fulfillment to the meaning of individual life. And since the kingdom of God lies beyond all the kingdoms of this world, the consideration of that divine realm is a challenge to preparation in the present order for a community life that shall be truly ultimate."[11] In a world without unity and love, "the key to a genuine recovery of historical Christian community may lie in the re-appropriation of a positive eschatology sprung out of Christian *agape*."[12]

The witness of the Church as a redemptive community also influences its social structure. Out of Israel and the pagan world alike, God is calling His sons into a real community-life through which the world is to be saved. Through the sharing of a common life and the surrender to a common purpose the Body is to spread over the face of the earth. The hope of the world, as Paul saw it, lay in the realization of the "Divine Commonwealth."[13] "Even so the historic drama of Christ's death and resurrection had brought into clear light the hidden purposes of God, by uniting faithful men, out of all nations and classes, in one firm commonwealth free and powerful to do the will of God."[14] Bonhoeffer has said that it is by seeing the cross and the community beneath it that men come to believe in God.[15] Dodd has summed up Paul's teaching on the Church as a community very cogently:

> That phrase (the Divine Commonwealth) represents Paul's "ecclesia of God." It is a community of loving persons, who bear one another's burdens, who seek to build up one another in love, who "have the same thoughts in relation to one another that they have in their communion with Christ." It is all this because it is the living embodiment of Christ's own Spirit. This is a high and mystical doctrine, but a doctrine which has no meaning apart from loving fellowship in real life. A company of

11. Petry, *Christian Eschatology and Social Thought*, p. 303.

12. Ibid., p. 380.

13. C. H. Dodd, *The Meaning of Paul for Today*. Dodd summarizes his findings on Paul in his preface as follows: "I find in Paul a religious philosophy of life oriented throughout to the idea of a society or commonwealth of God" (p. 7).

14. Ibid., p. 39.

15. Dietrich Bonhoeffer, *The Cost of Discipleship*, New York: Macmillan, 1949, p. 103.

people who celebrate a solemn sacrament of Christ's Body and Blood, and all the time are moved by selfish passions—rivalry, competition, mutual contempt—is not for Paul a Church or Divine Commonwealth at all, no matter how lofty their faith or how deep their mystical experience; for all these things may "puff up"; love alone "builds up."[16]

Anabaptism

Although Menno Simons never taught community of goods, there was in the Anabaptist movement in Switzerland and South Germany a real subordination of vocation and property to the purpose of the spread of the Kingdom. There was a singleness of purpose among the early Anabaptists, a total commitment that expressed itself in a sacrificial love that made a sharing brotherhood out of them. As craftsmen they traveled from city to city and from family to family opening the Kingdom for people to enter. They communicated a real revolution in the sense of priority: time, place, wealth, vocation, everything, must be subordinated to the spread of the Kingdom.

In a pre-Hutterite church discipline of 1527, the fourth article calls for a community of love: "every brother or sister shall yield himself in God to the brotherhood completely with body and life, and hold in common all gifts received of God."[17] A Strassburg Discipline of 1568 calls for a willingness to lay all that a person has (including money) on the altar and to let further economic issues be counseled within the brotherhood. Menno Simons, too, expressed the concern that wealth breaks the fellowship, and counseled a dedication of time and wealth to the brotherhood for the spread of the Gospel. In an unpublished study of the assimilation of the Dutch Mennonites in the seventeenth and eighteenth centuries, Irvin Horst has pointed out that accommodation and compromise first occurred in the field of economics. Once this inroad was made, the accommodation socially, intellectually, politically, and theologically followed in its path.

The Mennonites of America have, in general, taken an absolutist line in ethics. In the field of nonresistance they have maintained a fairly

---

16. Dodd, *The Meaning of Paul for Today*, p. 145.

17. Translated and edited by Robert Friedmann, "The Oldest Church Discipline of the Anabaptists," in *Mennonite Quarterly Review*, April, 1955, p. 164.

consistent position, but in the recent past they have been made aware of large areas of compromise in the field of economics. Whether the future will bring with it a relativity in political ethics to justify economic assimilation or whether the lines will be drawn tighter in the area of economics has yet to be seen. *If economic assimilation is harming the brotherhood and sapping the "body" of its vitality, a "better way" will have to be pioneered by a group that is willing to loosen its ties of economic involvement to subordinate "all things" to the purposes of the Kingdom.*

Conclusions

The Old Testament and New Testament are filled with warnings concerning covetousness and the piling up of earthly treasures. These warnings are valid because treasures keep men from entering the kingdom of God and threaten the community characteristics of the people of God.

The Jerusalem Church was moved by the Holy Spirit in love and justice to express its oneness of heart and soul in sharing material possessions. This was the voluntary expression of a deep spiritual unity.

The eschatological hope of early Christians caused them to look with indifference on the "things" of a world that was passing away. They realized that the past and present have their full significance only when viewed in the light of the future.

The spread of the redemptive community took precedence over vocation and the accumulation of possessions, and gave real meaning and content to the total commitment early Christians had made to Christ.

The divine love instilled in the members of the body—something the world does not have—seeks to express itself in a love community of mutual concern and sharing. *Agape* love alone can build up a Christian fellowship.

Christianity is not necessarily communistic in structure, but Christian love and discipleship always desire to share and bear the burdens and responsibilities of the others in the fellowship. In a materialistic society, the testimony of the Church might well involve a subordination of property to the purpose of the Church.

If wealth is a treasure on earth that keeps men from the kingdom of God, then it might once more be incumbent on the disciples of Christ to subordinate the possession and use of property to the church-brotherhood, so that once more there might be the oneness of heart and soul, the fellowship, the power, and the outreach of the first Church.

The Biblical record is not a story of the progressive emancipation of the individual but rather of God's action in history to create a redemptive community in which the transformed individual finds his true being. It is to this community that God through His Holy Spirit and the voice of His disciples is calling men today.

www.ingramcontent.com/pod-product-compliance
Lightning Source LLC
Chambersburg PA
CBHW031427150426
43191CB00006B/423